SAY IT LIKE IT MATTERS
WHEN IT MATTERS

PALMETTO
PUBLISHING
Charleston, SC
www.PalmettoPublishing.com

Say It Like It Matters When It Matters
Copyright © 2023 by Jeff Joiner

Hardcover ISBN: 979-8-8229-2772-8
Paperback ISBN: 979-8-8229-1938-9
eBook ISBN: 979-8-8229-2773-5

SAY IT LIKE IT MATTERS

WHEN IT MATTERS

COMMUNICATING WITH POWER, EFFECTIVENESS, AND AUTHENTICITY

JEFF JOINER

This book is dedicated to the most important people in my world, my extraordinary wife, Kathy, and my amazing kids, Amanda, Natalie, and Logan. I am humbled and honored by your love and support.

TABLE OF CONTENTS

INTRODUCTION

The day *is* coming.

The day you will be required to express yourself verbally in a situation where *a lot* is at stake.

Maybe you'll be sitting across from an important customer, standing behind a podium with a microphone in your hand, or on the most important interview of your life – but it's coming.

Those moments will continue to happen again and again throughout your life. The question is: ***Will you be prepared when those moments come?***

Your ability to put your ideas into words and deliver them with power, effectiveness, and authenticity when it matters will have so much to do with your success and happiness.

WHY I WROTE THIS BOOK

I've thought about writing a book for years, and I often get asked if I have one since most professional speakers do. But I've resisted the urge to write a book until now because it always seemed like an intrinsically egotistical thing to do – "You know what this world *really* needs? Another book! Full of *MY* ideas!"

But, over the years, I've seen so many people being held back in their lives, relationships, and careers because of their poor communication skills:

✦ Brilliant people who are afraid to share their ideas with others so no one will ever know how brilliant they are.

✦ Good people who want to help others, but can't, because what they say doesn't resonate with people.

✦ Honest people whom nobody trusts because they don't come across as authentic.

✦ Miserable people who are being bullied by difficult individuals because they don't know how to communicate with them effectively.

✦ Hard-working salespeople who only sell a fraction of what they should because they're going about it all wrong.

✦ Business owners with big dreams and great products who never seem to get off the ground because they don't connect with people.

✦ Individuals who would love to get up and speak at a loved one's funeral, wedding, or retirement party, but their paralyzing fear of public speaking keeps them frozen in their seats.

All of these people, and millions more like them, are struggling and suffering needlessly. *All* of them could change their lives and have extraordinary breakthroughs by learning to think differently about communication and developing some simple skills.

Everyone, including you, can learn to be a powerful, effective communicator.

My passion is teaching and equipping people to live victoriously and abundantly. With the book you're holding, I will do my very best to do that for you.

Authentic communication skills are more important than they've ever been. As people of all ages increasingly stare at their phones, human interaction skills are eroding worldwide. Artificial Intelligence is making people doubt the legitimacy of everything they read, and deepfake videos are causing them to question if it's real when they see someone speaking on video. We are moving into an era where people will only believe messages they see and hear people deliver live and in person.

In this book, I will share what I've learned to have breakthroughs in my life in crucial communication situations like public speaking, selling, interviewing, parenting, and dealing with difficult people. For each topic in this book, I'll help you learn the proper *mindset* required for success in that setting and some *skills* you can practice and master.

You must develop **both** the right **mindset** and **skill set** to be an effective communicator. Mindset and skill set are complementary and intertwined, like strategy and tactics. **One without the other is useless.** I will challenge you to **think differently** about what you are trying to accomplish and why and **to work on skills** that can be practiced and mastered.

I've been speaking about the topics in this book for thirty years. These ideas have set people free, enhanced their careers, and improved the quality of their lives. I hope they will do the same for you!

WHY LISTEN TO ME?

As my friends and family know all too well, I have opinions on *many* topics. But **communication** is the subject I have the most knowledge, experience, training, and credibility on.

I have a bachelor's degree in Communication Arts and a master's degree in Speech Communication. As a college student, I spent three years competing in intercollegiate speech competitions as a member of my university's speech team. I competed in events like Informative Speaking, Persuasive Speaking, Impromptu Speaking, Rhetorical Criticism, and Extemporaneous Speaking. That means, while all the normal kids were going to parties and football games, I was writing speeches, speaking in front of judges, learning to take some harsh critiques, developing my communication skills, practicing in front of a mirror, and giving more speeches.

In my senior year, I won first place in five different speaking events at the Ohio State Speech Championships, which was good enough to impress one of the judges (the Speech Communication Department Chair from Miami University) to offer me a full-ride scholarship to graduate school, where I would teach speech classes and help coach their speech team.

I earned my master's degree in less than a year and was offered a faculty position. I was twenty-two when I started teaching public speaking classes and coaching Miami's Speech Team to three state and two international championships.

As I'm sure you know, one of the best ways to master something is to teach it. Over one thousand students took my public speaking class, and I learned much more about effective communication by teaching it than doing it.

After five years, I left academia and worked in corporate business-to-business sales, where I had to learn and master an entirely different type of verbal communication – selling. I will go into the lessons I learned doing that and the breakthroughs I had in Section II of this book.

After ten years in sales, I spent another five years in corporate training, heading the Learning and Development department for a large regional sales organization. I learned how to coach communication skills in the business world, which differs entirely from a university environment. I taught a large sales force selling skills and provided speaking and training for hundreds of their client organizations.

In 2012, I went full-time into my own business that I had been running on the side for decades, launching *Jeff Joiner Training*. I have done conference keynote speaking and corporate employee training for over one thousand organizations in forty-nine U.S. states.

I also own another company where I teach people to start and operate a business of their own. This has required me to interview thousands of people and provide communication coaching to people with every possible personality type and skill set.

And most importantly, I have been married to my beautiful wife, Kathy, for 32 years and counting, and we have three exceptional adult children. Even with my extensive academic and corporate experience, I've learned the most important lessons about effective communication at home!

I don't claim to be the world's most prominent expert on communication skills. But I have done it a lot, probably more than anyone you know or have ever met. And I've helped hundreds of others learn how to communicate with more power, authenticity, and effectiveness.

PREVIEW

There are three parts to this book. *Part I* will focus on **public speaking**. You'll learn the mindset of influential speakers and then some skills you can and should practice and develop. *Part II* is all about **selling**, covering the mindset of world-class salespeople and the communication skills you can develop to succeed in sales. *Part III* digs into communicating in six different types of **essential conversations**: With strangers, in interviews, with difficult people, in relationships, with your kids, and to yourself.

You have brilliant ideas in that head of yours! Ideas that could help you, your friends, your family, and your co-workers succeed at a higher level and live happier, more fulfilling lives. Ideas that could help your customers reach and exceed their goals. Ideas that could change the world. Keep reading, and I will do my best to help you *say it like it matters when it matters!*

PUBLIC SPEAKING

If you want to advance in your career, grow your business, or have more respect for the person you see in the mirror, I can't think of a better strategy than to improve your public speaking ability. It's high on the list of things most people can't do very well and an ability people universally respect.

This section will focus on the mindset required for confident, effective public speaking and some skills you can develop, practice, and master.

CHAPTER 1

THE IMPORTANCE OF DEVELOPING YOUR PUBLIC SPEAKING ABILITY

Verbal communication is the backbone of society and life. It's what separates us from animals. Well, that and we're not afraid of vacuum cleaners.

Public speaking has *always* been critical. It's been the primary way throughout history that individuals earned respect, gained a following, and made a difference in the world. Cicero, Socrates, Jesus, Sojourner Truth, Abraham Lincoln, Susan B. Anthony, Queen Elizabeth I, Winston Churchill, John F. Kennedy, Mohandas Gandhi, Margaret Thatcher, and Ronald Reagan were all individuals who changed the world, mainly because of their ability to communicate publicly.

When I moved into my faculty office in the Speech Communication Department at Miami University, the only things besides a desk, chair, filing cabinet, and bookshelf were a few old, dusty books on public speaking that no one wanted. When I left there five years later, I snatched those old books and have them in my library today. One of the oldest is *A First Course in Public Speaking*, by James A. Winans and Hoyt H. Hudson, professors in the 1920s at Dartmouth College and Princeton University. In it, they wrote,

> "We venture the assertion that public speaking was never before a larger element in the success of the individual and in the conduct of the affairs of society than at the present time, and that, whatever changes may come in the means and methods of communication, the demand for good talking, in public and in private, will continue so great as to justify special training for some millennia to come."

Over one hundred years ago, they predicted that the demand for effective public speaking would justify special training into the future, and they certainly nailed it. Public speaking skills are vital in almost every field in today's workplace.

The Graduate Management Admission Council publishes a study annually based on survey responses from nearly one thousand corporate recruiters and staffing firms. In their 2022 publication, they reported that ***interpersonal skills*** are the most important thing for candidates for MBA-level positions in the U.S. to possess. Those skills ranked higher than other crucial skills like learning, motivation, leadership, strategy and innovation, decision-making, and strategic and systems skills.

Communication skills aren't just what employers are looking for; they are what workers say helps them the most in the workplace. According to a study by sociologist Andrew Zekeri, "Oral communication skills are the number one skill that college graduates find useful in the business world."

If you own a small business, public speaking skills are even more critical. You most likely won't be able to rely on traditional advertising to grow your business. Your most powerful tool will be your ability to articulate your ideas effectively in the marketplace, to your team, and to the world.

You use public speaking skills more frequently than you think. I'm not just talking about speeches behind a podium with a microphone. In his book *The Exceptional Presenter*, Timothy J. Koegel rightly said, "Every time you open your mouth to speak in public, you are a public speaker. Whenever you utter a phrase within earshot of another human being, you make an impression." That impression could be very valuable or very costly.

When I do public speaking training for corporate executives and business owners, I ask them a question.

True or False:

Ten minutes spent *effectively sharing the right information* with the *right audience* could mean more to your business than an entire year sitting at your desk.

The unanimous answer is always ***true***. Your ability to effectively organize and present your ideas to others will profoundly impact your career success.

Let's look at some of the many benefits that will come when you focus on improving your public speaking ability:

- ✦ *Improving speaking skills boosts confidence.* There are few things I have seen that make people feel sky-high more than nailing a presentation. In the next chapter, I will help you learn to overcome fear so your confidence will soar quickly!

- ✦ *Public speaking gives you an increased ability to think critically.* As you learn to organize and express your ideas effectively, you'll become a better consumer of other people's ideas. Learning what works to persuade and influence others will help you better discern the reliability of the messages intended to influence you.

- ✦ *Effective public speaking builds trust.* Many studies have shown that people are more likely to trust someone who can express their ideas well in front of others. For people to trust you, you must be trust***worthy***; your ability to communicate is one of the many ways you project that to others.

- ✦ *Public speaking skills help you stand for what you believe in*. If you have strong views about issues and ideas (and if you're a decent person, you do), you're going to want to be able to win people over to your point of view. Strong views without strong speaking skills don't change much of anything.
- ✦ *You'll gain the ability to inspire others*. Your story might be the key to someone else's breakthrough. But if you can't express it effectively to others, your life story will be like a tree falling in the woods with no one there to hear it.

The bottom line is that investing time and energy into improving your speaking ability in public is crucial. If you are like most people, the main thing holding you back is *fear*. But that's easier to overcome than you probably think.

CHAPTER 2

OVERCOMING FEAR OF PUBLIC SPEAKING

I'm sure you have heard that public speaking is the number one fear of people worldwide. Even more than fear of death, which is hard to believe. According to the National Institute of Mental Health, 75% of people say public speaking when asked about their biggest fear. Number two on the list is death. Jerry Seinfeld famously joked, "That means, to the average person, if you have to be at a funeral, you would rather be *in the casket* than doing the eulogy."

It's a funny line, but it reflects a profoundly sad reality. If you let fear of public speaking slow you down, cause stress, or limit your career options, it's time to stop.

I've seen people go to extraordinary lengths to avoid public speaking because of fear and people who let their fear get the best of them. When I was teaching public speaking classes to college students, I saw a kid get so nervous and panicked that he passed out and hit the floor like a falling tree (he was ok, but it was scary for everyone!). Another student got mixed up and a little tongue-tied. He took a deep breath, turned, and walked out the door. He left his backpack at his desk and never came back. Not just that day - but for the rest of the semester! I tried to contact him, but he wouldn't return my calls. I eventually gave him an "Incomplete" on his report card because I didn't want to fail him for being afraid. Two years later, the Registrar's Office made me assign him a letter grade, and I had to give him an "F" - the only kid I ever failed.

My wife Kathy, a powerful conference speaker today, was so nervous about getting up and speaking in her college speech class that she took a zero instead of speaking when it was her turn. (She's come a long way!).

I've seen people quit jobs, turn down promotions, drop out of classes, change majors, hide in bathrooms, or leave their own businesses – all because of their fear of public speaking.

It's tragically sad to me because of all the fears you could have, it's one of the easiest to defeat. It breaks my heart that so many people live less-than-ideal lives because no one has shown them how to conquer that fear. It's part of the reason I'm writing this book – to help people free themselves from their self-imposed torment. Let's look at why people are so afraid of public speaking, what they're *really* afraid of, and how you can ensure you are never scared of public speaking again.

WHY SO AFRAID?

I'm not saying that I don't understand why people are afraid of public speaking; I get it. I'm saying that if you are scared, you've **trapped yourself** in a negative thought cycle.

According to psychotherapist Dr. Pat LaDouceur:

> "For some people, the roots of a fear of public speaking are buried deep in our past. For example, the fear can come from an experience where we were once embarrassed or ridiculed or even overwhelmed with attention that was supposed to be positive.
>
> For others, the roots of their fear of public speaking are in an adult performance that didn't go well...or didn't seem to go well. When you perform again, the worrisome memories come back to haunt you. They generate thoughts like, 'I'm going to blow it,' 'I don't belong here,' 'What if they don't like me?' and so forth.
>
> Either way, to the survival part of our brain, the situation looks dangerous. Your body gets ready to fight, flee, or freeze, which means physical tension, shaking, increased blood pressure, rapid heartbeat, sweating, and forgetting what you were about to say. Once in motion, the cycle of fear builds on itself."

The human body is such a fascinating thing. When you encounter a stressful situation, your body dumps adrenaline and cortisol into your bloodstream, and an extraordinary process kicks into gear. Your heart rate increases to pump blood to your arms and legs in case you need to fight or run. Your digestive system instantly shuts down, making you feel butterflies in your stomach and a dry mouth. Your body triggers eccrine sweat glands, which are most dense in your palms and the soles of your feet, to produce sweat to cool your body down. That's why you get sweaty palms. (You have probably never noticed your feet sweating when you're speaking, too, but they do!).

But here's what you must understand – all that is *perfectly natural*. That's how your body was designed to work, and it's fantastic.

It's identical to how your body acts when you're excited! Like when your team is about to kick the winning field goal during the big game, or you're going in for that first kiss. *The key is how you think about those natural physiological responses*. You can interpret the butterflies, sweat, and racing heart as proof that you are a frightened loser about to crash and burn, or you can interpret those responses as an indication that you are excited about the opportunity to share your ideas with others.

That sounds overly simple, but it really is as simple as that. You commit to a negative downward spiral if you go the fear and anxiety path. You notice the sweat, racing heart, etc., and think, "Oh no! I'm freaking out. I'm so nervous! I hate public speaking! This is a bad idea! I wish I were anywhere else!" Unfortunately, thoughts like that INCREASE the stress, which in turn causes more adrenaline, more sweat, etc., which increases the pressure even more, and now you're doomed to a bad presentation.

The micro-spiral of that event is bad enough, but it leads to a macro-cycle over time. After you sit down, you think, "See? I'm terrible at speaking. I hate it. It's something I'm just not good at. I'm an idiot." The next time you're asked to speak somewhere, the whole process repeats, but it's even worse now, further cementing your opinion that you're a terrible speaker.

After this happens a few times, it gets so bad that people start saying things like they'd rather die than give a speech. It gets *even worse* when people begin to look at it as a ***phobia*** because a phobia is a disorder, right? A disease? It's something you were born with, right? ***So, it's not your fault***.

When people get to this point, they accept their fear of public speaking as something they can't control and can't change. They embrace it as part of their personality - part of their *identity* - how they see themselves.

All of that is very sad because it **CAN** be controlled, and it **CAN** be changed. I'm not a psychologist, but I have worked with hundreds of people who have turned this around and banished their fear of speaking for good. Everyone I've ever worked with who opened themselves up for some coaching and sincerely tried has overcome their fear of speaking. ***Everyone***.

Until this point in your life, it hasn't been your fault if you suffer from fear of public speaking. No one has taught you how to overcome your fears, so you've been victimized by your own runaway thought process. But, after today, if you continue to suffer from fear of public speaking, it ***will*** be your fault because you are choosing to cling to an old way of thinking after learning how to set yourself free. It would be like some-one released from prison continuing to sit in their cell. That's about as sad as it gets.

Before getting into my recommendations to kick your fear to the curb, we must be honest with each other about what you're truly afraid of.

THE TRUE FEAR UNMASKED

You're not *really* afraid of public speaking. Nobody is. It's not danger-ous. It's unlikely that you will fall off the stage or get electrocuted by the microphone, and no one will sneak up behind you and grab you. I've spoken in front of thousands of audiences, and no one has ever come up and punched me or even thrown tomatoes.

People say, "Well, I'm afraid of screwing up and doing a bad job." Now you're getting warmer, but that's still not it. You are just as likely, if not more so, to screw up when sending an email, shipping boxes, or analyz-ing the budgets, all activities you do much more frequently. You screw up many times a day without fear gripping your heart.

What you're concerned might happen is that you'll do or say some-thing that *makes you look bad*.

This means you're truly afraid of *other people's opinions about you*.

That's it. All of this, the alleged "biggest fear in the world" tormenting 75% of humanity, boils down to the fact that *you care too much about what other people think of you*.

Remember back in middle school when you were obsessed with trying to be cool and wishing you were popular? All your decisions, from the clothes and hairstyles you wore to the music you listened to, were driven by what other people thought of you. That's natural when you're 13 and still trying to figure out who you are. But you're supposed to grow out of that. You're an adult now, and this is still an issue? It's time to **grow up** and **let it go**. If you want to be an effective speaker, or an effective anything, or a happy person for that matter – you will have to **stop caring so much about what other people think**.

The people who love you will still love you no matter what you say in your presentation. The people who don't like you and the negative, critical people will find something to criticize no matter what you say or how you say it. So let it go.

I love a quote attributed to many people, but it's powerful: "What other people think of you is none of your business."

Your obsession with what other people think of you is the root of your public speaking anxiety (and many other problems, but those are topics for another book).

So how do you change it?

IT'S NOT ABOUT YOU

A friend of mine, who is brilliant, but not a compelling speaker, asked me for advice on how he could be a better speaker. He noticed that when he is scheduled to present next at a conference, many people get up to go to the restroom. He also saw that people don't do that when I'm up next. (Interesting observation, and he's right).

I asked him to finish this sentence: "After I'm done speaking, I hope people know _____(blank)_____."

Without missing a beat, he said, "How smart I am! I hope they know how smart I am!"

"Well, mission accomplished, dude," I said. "Everyone knows you're smart. But *no one benefits* from listening to you demonstrate your intelligence for twenty minutes. It's just a waste of everyone's time. No one came to this event hoping to be astonished by your genius."

I told him how *I* would finish the fill-in-the-blank sentence: "After I'm done speaking, I hope people know how amazing and capable of greatness *they* are, not how great *I am*."

The difference between those two intentions is the difference between *boring* and *riveting*, *useless* and *useful*, and *mediocre* and *extraordinary*.

And it's the key to turning everything around.

GET YOUR HEART RIGHT

When someone who has a "fear of public speaking" gets up in front of an audience to speak, or even *thinks* about doing that, while adrenaline is flooding their bloodstream, their *mind* is being flooded with *thoughts* like these:

✦ "I hope I don't blow this."

✦ "Everyone is staring at me."

✦ "I hope I don't sound like an idiot."

✦ "Is my voice too high?"

✦ "I bet they can see the sweat in my armpits."

✦ "Some people aren't even paying attention to me."

✦ "How long have I been talking? Too long? Too short?"

✦ "That didn't come out like I wanted it to."

✦ "I forgot what I wanted to say. I AM an idiot."

✦ "I'm so embarrassed."

✦ "I'm terrible at this."

✦ "People hate me."

And on and on and on. At lightning speed, stress-inducing, humiliating, shameful, soul-crushing thoughts about themselves start to pound them like torpedoes, sinking their presentation and self-confidence. What do all the above thoughts have in common?

"I... me... I... I... my... I... my... me... I... I... I... I... I'm... I'm... me..."

YOU'RE FOCUSED ON THE WRONG THING! Why are you so focused on yourself? That's the whole problem! You've set yourself up to do poorly by concentrating on the *opposite* thing from what you should be thinking about. It's like you've pointed 1,000 glaring spotlights in your face, burning you alive!

It's not about you! At least it shouldn't be!

Here's what **powerful speakers** who communicate with effectiveness and authenticity are thinking before they speak and while they are speaking:

+ "What an exciting opportunity to share this information with others."

+ "This is going to help people."

+ "How can I explain this idea in a way that impacts people?"

+ "Look! Someone's taking notes! They must be getting something out of this."

+ "I just saw a lightbulb go off in that woman's mind! I saw it on her face! How awesome is that?"

+ "I'm so grateful for the chance to make a difference today."

Do you see the *HUGE* difference? You may still get some butterflies and sweaty palms, but you need to immediately chalk it up to the *excitement* you're feeling about your opportunity to talk about something that matters and helps people understand something they didn't understand before!

Thinking about helping, serving, blessing, informing, ministering, preparing, or equipping people in the audience instead of thinking about yourself causes fear and anxiety to melt away. The sweat stops, you gain momentum, the shame is replaced with pride and confidence, and that negative spiral is inverted into a positive spiral that culminates in an excellent experience for everyone!

Some of you think, "It can't be that simple." It is. I'm telling you, it is. Like Marcus Aurelius said, "The happiness of your life depends on the quality of your thoughts."

What you are suffering from isn't "fear of public speaking." It's a bad case of **self-centered, self-absorbed selfishness**. And you can change it instantly by thinking less about yourself and more about being a blessing to others.

Humility isn't thinking less of yourself. It's thinking of yourself **less**.

When you think about using your speaking as an opportunity to **give**, you show **love**, the most powerful force in the universe. That is the secret to communicating with power, **to ensure that your purpose is helping others**.

I didn't make this up, by the way. I'm sure people from different spiritual and religious backgrounds are reading this book, but I'm a Christian. Jesus talked about this when he said, "There is no fear in love, but perfect love casts out fear." Applying this verse to public speaking might be somewhat unconventional, but I think it's perfect! When you do something loving, like trying to help the people in the audience learn something or change something in their life, you're **casting fear out the door** because there is nothing to be afraid of!

This is why I am never nervous when speaking to an audience. Because no matter the topic or situation, I'm not there for me! I'm there for the people in the audience.

It's also why I never do something most people do at the end of their presentation. I never say, "Thank you" or "Thank you for your time." Never. That's just not how I look at what's going on. I did my best to say things that made a difference in the audience's lives. I'm doing everything I can to help them learn to be happier, more productive, less stressed people. If anything, *they* should be thanking *me*! (Which they do when they clap at the end). It would be more appropriate to end by saying, "You're welcome!" but I don't think everyone would understand.

Here are a few other things you can do to feel less nervous when you're speaking in public:

Be Thoroughly Prepared. One way to reduce any lingering nervousness is to ensure you are prepared. Knowing more about the topic I'm discussing than anyone in the room gives me confidence. That's one of the reasons I tell stories about things that have happened to me in my own life. No one on Earth is a more prominent expert on the topic of my life than I am!

Give Yourself a Pep-Talk. When I started as a speaker, I would go in the bathroom and tell the guy in the mirror how awesome he was. I'd give myself a pep-talk like a coach before the big game! Your sub-conscious mind believes whatever you tell it about yourself, so I programmed mine to think that I was confident and articulate! It worked! More on how to do that in Chapter 30.

Don't Forget – They Don't Know. I talked about this subject with my 18-year-old son Logan, who is an excellent public speaker. He has started two successful YouTube channels and has spoken in front of groups of several hundred people. He said, "The key for me is remembering that the people in the audience have no idea what I meant to say or what I forgot to say. They don't know." That is some wisdom right there!

Yawn. This is a trick I learned years ago when I was doing speech competitions. These were high-pressure situations where you were competing directly against other good speakers and getting ranked and evaluated by judges. (Imagine if a judge gave you a score and a writ-ten critique every time you expressed yourself at work!). Something I found would release tension and help me relax was *yawning*. Before speaking, I'd cut loose with a few big, stretch-your-arms-out yawns and feel great! I didn't realize why it worked; I just knew it did.

I learned later that yawning cools and cleans your brain. Yawning gets cerebral-spinal fluid flowing and activates the lymphatic system.

It releases neurotransmitters like dopamine (responsible for allowing you to feel pleasure, satisfaction, and motivation) and serotonin (which regulates mood, appetite, sleep, muscle contraction, and some cognitive functions like learning and memory).

So, next time you're stressed, bust out a few yawns and see if you don't feel better! I bet you've never heard that advice before.

Now that you know some strategies to eliminate fear, let's look at ways to *connect with your audience*.

CHAPTER 3

CONNECTING WITH THE AUDIENCE

One of the most crucial aspects of effective public speaking is connecting with your audience. If you are not able to do that, you're sunk.

In his book *Everyone Communicates, Few Connect*, John C. Maxwell said,

> "Connecting is the ability to identify with people and relate to them in a way that increases your influence with them. Why is that important? Because the ability to communicate and connect with others is a major determining factor in reaching your full potential. To be successful, you must work with others. And to do that at your absolute best, you must learn to connect."

Connecting with audience members starts with understanding *who* and *what* you are.

Do you know that your body isn't you? Your body is an extraordinary temperature-regulating, blood-pumping, food-digesting, oxygen-breathing, reproducing, muscle-contracting, chemical-producing, self-healing machine! It's an incredibly complex system of bones, veins, glands, organs, muscles, nerves, joints, tendons, cartilage, tissue, and hair that automatically accomplishes millions of daily tasks and duties.

It's truly miraculous, and you better take of your body because it's the only one you're getting during your lifetime on Earth.

*But it's not **who you are**.*

You are a spirit. You have a soul (your mind, will, and emotions – your personality), and you live in a body.

As impressive as it is, your body is simply the ***vehicle for the real you*** – your spirit.

Your spirit is what loves others, yearns to make a difference, is where you feel true peace and joy, and, I believe, is the part of you that will live forever, long after your body turns to dust.

It's your spirit that connects with other people. Have you ever noticed that hearing someone speak live is more impactful than a recording or a video conference call? Or that hearing music live at a concert is more powerful than a recording? That's because the speaker or musician is a spirit, and you are a spirit, and you are connecting on a spiritual level. And it's powerful.

This all might sound a little corny, but I guarantee you've felt it. I'd bet you've met someone before and felt they were giving off a bad vibe, so you mistrusted them or stayed away. I'm sure you've also met people you were instantly drawn to, feeling like you were kindred spirits. The spirit-to-spirit connection can happen when speaking one-on-one with somebody or a group.

Let me give you two examples that happened to me two days in a row. On a Saturday some years ago, I was sitting at a restaurant having lunch with friends during a break at a conference in Cincinnati. A man we didn't know walked up to our table with a young girl as we ate and talked. I *IMMEDIATELY* knew that he was going to ask us for some money. You could see it in his eyes. You could feel it. And, sure enough, he apologized for interrupting and told us that he ran out of gas and that he and his little girl needed some money to get home to Lexington. I gave him twenty bucks and wished him well, not knowing if he was scamming us. I figure, be a giver, and good things will happen, and either way, I hope things got better for that dude. But the point is how *obvious it was to my spirit* that his spirit was **taking**.

The next day, I was meeting some friends at an amusement park for a day of roller coasters and fun. While waiting for our friends to meet us outside the front entrance, a woman came walking up to me and said, "Excuse me …" I *IMMEDIATELY* could sense that she was about to give me something. You could see it in her eyes. You could feel it. And, sure enough, she said, "Have you purchased your tickets yet? We have four extra tickets for today that we won't use, and you can have them if you want." We thanked her and told her we already had season passes to the park but were blown away by her kindness. We watched as she found a family with young kids to bless with those tickets. But, again, my spirit could feel her spirit and knew that she was *giving*.

The same thing occurs when speaking to an audience. They can feel your spirit and know if you're full of it or being truthful. The people in the audience can tell if you're there to take or to give and can feel if you're being real or fake.

Probably the most unexpected advice you'll get in a book about communication is that if you want to be more effective, you must get your heart right. If you want to improve your results in presenting, one of the best ways is to work on improving yourself as a person. The nice thing about this advice is that it doesn't take talent or even skill but a sincere desire to be a better person and make a difference in the lives of others. It will also improve communication in all your relationships.

In addition to connecting with people's spirits, you can connect with their souls - their minds, wills, and emotions. Daniel Goleman explains in his book *Social Intelligence, the New Science of Human Relationships*, "We are wired to connect. Neuroscience has discovered that our brain's very design makes it sociable, inexorably drawn into an intimate brain-to-brain linkup whenever we engage with another person. That neural bridge lets us affect the brain – and so the body – of everyone we interact with, just as they do us."

Effective communication is all about connecting. If you want to get better at connecting with your audience, here are some things I recommend:

Be Yourself. I know that advice can sound trite, but we've all been guilty of trying to impress people by being something we're not. Never is the temptation to do that stronger than when speaking in public.

Pretending to be someone you're not is a fool's errand. First, it's exhausting. It takes enormous mental energy to convince people that you are something other than the person you are. Ask a professional actor how tired they are at the end of the day. When speaking in public, you need all the mental capacity you can muster focused on delivering a message that matters.

You're also setting yourself up for unavoidable disappointment. Even if your presentation went great and people loved you, they didn't love *you*, and you know it. They loved the person you were pretending to be. This will crush your sense of self-worth and send you down a spiraling path of misery the more you speak in front of others.

When you try to be something or someone you're not, you are depriving the world of the one thing you ***can be*** better than anyone – ***you***. You were asked or invited to speak at that event for a reason, and people want to hear from you, not some phony version of you that you think is more appealing.

And the worst problem is, you're not fooling anybody. People can tell. And on the list of traits people can't stand, being fake is high on the list. Strive for authenticity, which to me means that the "inside you" and the "outside you" are the same "you."

Remember That You're Not Better Than Anyone in the Audience. You may be more intelligent, better educated, or more experienced than the people in your audience. I hope you are better informed on the topic you're speaking on than they are. ***But you're not better than them.*** When a speaker tries to sound intelligent or clever or like the world's leading expert on a topic, they usually appear arrogant to the audience. The quickest way to alienate yourself from the audience is to create the impression that you feel superior to them.

People play different roles in different situations. Sometimes you're the speaker, and sometimes you're in the audience. In my relationship with you, I am currently in the role of writer, and you are in the role of reader. I probably have a lot more experience than you do with communication and public speaking, which defines our roles. But there are numerous topics you know more about than I do, and if a book were to be written on any of those topics, the roles would be reversed, and I'd be reading your expert advice! I'm not better than you are, and you're not better than I am. We're both trying to learn and grow and do things that matter. That's the same approach I have when I speak to an audience. We're all in this together, and I'm sharing what I know, hoping it is valuable to you.

Use Humor, but Be Smart About It. Showing a sense of humor is a great way to keep your presentation interesting and connecting with the audience. A 2017 study published in the *Journal of Personality and Social Psychology* found that the successful use of humor increases status and perceptions of confidence and competence and plays a fundamental role in shaping interpersonal perceptions and hierarchies within groups.

But you must be watchful. Attempting humor while giving a presentation can be risky business. Everyone has a different idea of what's funny, and the list of topics someone might find offensive is growing exponentially. We'll talk about the skill of using humor in Chapter 8.

Smile and Laugh. If you look like you're not enjoying yourself, no one else will enjoy themselves. Put a smile on your face, lighten up, and have fun.

Don't be Afraid to Talk About Things That Matter. I'm sure you've heard you should never publicly discuss certain topics, like religion or politics. That advice is cowardly, and those same people spend all their time gossiping about others, which is much less wise than talking about religion or politics. ***It's always ok to talk about ideas, especially significant ones.*** Just don't be a jerk about it. I love what Eleanor Roosevelt said, "Great minds discuss ideas; average minds discuss events; small minds discuss people."

You'll have to address sensitive topics sometimes if you ever hope to make a difference with your life. If everything you said while speaking publicly were things that everyone already knew and agreed with, then what's the point of the meeting? What a waste of time. If I want to help people, I will have to nudge them out of their comfort zone and occasionally say things that step on their toes. But I don't shove them out of their comfort zone or ***stomp*** on their toes.

I never tell people what to believe, but with lots of authentic humility, I share what I have found to be true and valuable in my life. I often talk about topics like faith versus fear, thankfulness, standards of excellence, happiness, creating a culture of honor, extending grace to others, how to have peace and joy, not taking offense, aligning your decisions with your beliefs and goals, the power of love, and taking your eyes off yourself and serving others. People appreciate it when a speaker talks about things that matter, and it stands out because it's rare - especially in the workplace.

Look People in the Eye. In Section III of this book, I'll address the powerful role that eye contact plays in one-on-one interpersonal conversations, but it's powerful in public speaking, too. You may have heard this terrible advice: If you are nervous, look above the heads of the people, and look at the back of the room. That will only make you *more* nervous because doing that doesn't make people disappear. They are still there, and you are blowing it. (The only worse speaking advice is to picture the audience naked. You haven't looked at too many audiences if you think that's a good idea).

I look at as many people in the eye as I can when I speak. If there are 50 people or less in a room, I look each of them right in the eyes at least once during my talk. If there are hundreds of people, I pick someone from each section of the room to look in the eye. If there are thousands of people, you are on a stage with spotlights in your eyes, and eye contact is impossible (which is a lot more difficult for me).

Don't hop, hop, hop from one person's eyes to another like Frogger trying to get across the road. Pick a person and look them in the eyes while you speak a sentence or two. And then move on to someone else. It keeps people's attention and prevents them from drifting off if they think you might look them in the eye any second. It also makes each person in the audience feel like they are having a personal conversation with you, not listening to someone give a speech.

Interact with the Audience as Much as Possible. Get interaction going with the people in the audience. If it's a small group, say 30 or less, asking people to contribute is very effective. Ask questions and let people share what they think. If it's a large audience, I ask a lot of "Raise your hand if ..." questions to keep people engaged. My rule for asking questions is: Never ask a question unless you know exactly what the answer will be, or it doesn't matter what the answer is.

When I was teaching college speech classes, a student gave a persuasive speech about the dangers of nuclear energy. He started his speech by asking the class, "Who would be comfortable if a nuclear power plant were built in your hometown?" assuming no one would raise their hand. He didn't know that during the previous class (which he skipped), another student gave an excellent persuasive speech on nuclear power's safety, usefulness, and cost-effectiveness. So, when he asked his question, everyone raised their hand. He was shocked and flustered and never recovered, but he provided me with a teachable moment for the class, and I doubt he ever did that again!

Use Names Often. In one of the best-selling books of all time, written almost 90 years ago, *How to Win Friends and Influence People*, Dale Carnegie wrote, "Remember that a person's name is to that person, the sweetest and most important sound in any language." Don't overdo it, but calling people in the audience by their name, if you know them, keeps things personal and helps you connect with people.

Connecting with the audience is essential but a means to an end. Next, we'll discuss what you are ***trying to accomplish*** in your presentation.

CHAPTER 4

WHAT'S THE POINT?

One of the biggest things that stops people from becoming powerful and influential speakers is that they have no idea what they are trying to accomplish. Someone asks them to speak at a meeting or conference, and usually, the speaker is assigned a topic. Maybe they're asked to discuss growing business sales volume, leadership skills, cyber security, third-quarter projections, or whatever. So, they research, review the notes they've taken when other people have spoken about that topic in the past, and then get up and share as much information about that topic as they can think of—the end.

That presentation will almost certainly be dull and forgettable, and nothing will have changed in the audience's minds, hearts, or lives.

One morning at a conference, one of my friends asked me for advice. He is an extraordinary person, an incredible husband and father, and a tremendous leader, but he's not yet a great speaker.

He said, "Jeff, I'm speaking at the conference tonight! Do you have any advice?"

My first thought was that waiting until the day of the conference to ask for advice might be a little late, but at least he's asking. (That's how I know he'll be a great speaker someday because he's trying to get better, and his success in business means he'll get lots of opportunities to practice).

I told him, "I do have some advice that might help. I would challenge you to think about the difference between *talking about a subject* and *making a point*."

He thought briefly and said, "I didn't know there *was* a difference."

He would talk *about* a topic for fifteen or twenty minutes. It wasn't *effective* – couldn't be effective – because there was no objective or purpose.

You must have a *point*. Why are you talking? What are you trying to accomplish? What is the purpose? Ralph C. Smedley, the founder of the international speakers organization Toastmasters International said, "A speech without a purpose is like a journey without a destination."

I am challenging you, no matter the topic, to ensure you are making *some point*. It doesn't matter to me what that point is, but if you don't have one, your presentation is literally *pointless*!

I ran across a great old passage about this from the 1700s. Scottish minister and rhetorician Hugh Blair said, "Whenever a man speaks or writes, he is supposed, as a rational being, to have some end in view: either to inform, or to amuse, or to persuade, or, in some way or other, to act upon his fellow creatures. He who speaks or writes in such a manner as to adapt all his words most effectively to that end is the most eloquent man."

A little more modern perspective on this topic comes from the classic 1987 movie *Planes, Trains, and Automobiles*, when Neal Page (played by Steve Martin) tells Dell Griffith (played by John Candy), "You know when you're telling these little stories? Here's a good idea: ***Have a point!*** It makes it so much more interesting for the listener!"

I know this advice sounds rudimentary, but you *wouldn't believe* how often I've heard someone speak for 15 minutes, 30 minutes, or sometimes hours without making a point. Sometimes it's a little interesting, and sometimes even funny, but it's ***ineffective***. It doesn't move the needle; nothing changes because of their talk.

So, here's my advice on making a point:

Begin With the End in Mind. One of the books that changed my life for the better was the international bestseller, *The Seven Habits of Highly Effective People*, by Stephen Covey. Habit #2 in the book is "Begin with The End in Mind." The idea is that you must imagine and visualize what you want the end result of your work to be at the beginning of the process.

This has been a critical success principle for some of the most accomplished people. Many of the most successful business owners I know started their careers as engineers. I'm convinced it's because engineers don't start a project without having schematics, blueprints, drawings, or plans, and they don't quit halfway through a project! They are great at building things, which often includes a business.

An effective presentation needs to be built too. In Chapter 6, I'll cover how to make an outline and structure a presentation, but here's the big picture of how I decide what I'm going to talk about when I speak somewhere, in this order:

1) *What do I want people to __DO__ after I'm done speaking?* Maybe you want people to have more confidence selling products, get involved in a charity project, commit to being a better teammate in the workplace, vote for a particular political candidate, or work more effectively in their own businesses – whatever. *That's where you start.* What action do you want to encourage, challenge, and inspire people to take?

2) *What do people need to __FEEL__ to make them want to __DO__ that thing?* People are emotional creatures, and they almost always do what they feel like doing when they feel like doing it. You won't say anything that makes people more focused, disciplined, or kind. You're not a magician, and you can't change people. But you *can* spark or initiate feelings inside people that *make them want* to be more focused, disciplined, or kind.

I sometimes do personalized coaching for business professionals. Once, a high-level corporate executive hired me to coach him to be a better speaker. He was a brilliant finance guy but was very ineffective at driving change in the multi-billion-dollar organization where he worked, and he knew it. His excuse was - and I bet you've heard this phrase before – "You can lead a horse to water, but you can't make them drink." Disappointed, I said, "You don't get it at all. Your job as a leader and speaker isn't to make them *drink*. It's to make them *thirsty*."

Instead of forcing people to change, which is an impossible, exhausting, foolish objective, focus on ways you can make people *want* to change, which is very doable.

3) ***What do I need to <u>SAY</u> that might make them <u>FEEL</u> that way?***
You may need to tell a story about somebody, just like them, who made a change, and it was worth it. Maybe you need to share something personal about your life and what you did to have a breakthrough. You may need to build a dream for them and paint a vision for what is possible if they take some action. Maybe you need to raise their belief with some success stories of others living their dreams. You may need to share some compelling statistics. Perhaps you need to predict their future if they take action AND if they don't. Or a thousand other possible ideas, but your decisions on what you say and how you say it should be strategic and aligned with the end in mind.

So,

1) *What do I want people to **DO** after I'm done speaking?*

2) *What do people need to **FEEL** to make them want to **DO** that thing?*

3) *What do I need to **SAY** that might make them **FEEL** that way?*

If you follow those steps for deciding what to say and how to say it, not only is your talk the one people are most likely to pay attention to and remember, but you have a legitimate chance of helping the people in your audience live better lives and accomplish extraordinary things. And that's an incredible feeling.

Borrow Credibility. It's unlikely that you are the world's leading expert on very many topics, and neither am I. That's why I borrow credibility from people who ***are experts***. A great strategy to help you make your point is to quote books, articles, movies, famous credible people, scientific studies, and people perceived as experts by your audience. By doing this, you are ***adding weight*** to your arguments, which helps you make your point. You'll notice that I am doing that throughout this book. It's a powerful way to make your words more compelling to the audience.

Next, I'll address the part of this thing that no one wants to do – ***practice***.

CHAPTER 5

WE TALKING ABOUT PRACTICE?

As a sports fan and a student of public speaking, you can imagine how much I enjoy the drama and nonsense that comes from players and coaches doing press conferences with the media. These people were hired for their athletic and game-planning abilities, not their communication skills, so the results are often cringy and hilarious.

When I was running the speech team at Miami University, the Athletic Director called my office and asked me if I was willing to provide some public speaking training for the head coaches of every sports team on campus. He said, "If any employee of this university is likely to get a TV camera stuck in their face and asked difficult questions, it's these folks. And they are ***not*** good at it." And he was right. One of the funniest memories of my strange career was walking into a room where all the head coaches were sitting with their chairs in a circle. What made it funny was that each coach was dressed completely differently from the others, all in the styles of their sport. The athletic director introduced me and my credentials and then asked the coaches to go around and introduce themselves. "Wait!" I said, "Let me see if I can guess based on your outfit. Short shorts, high socks, and whistle – football! White sweater with sleeves draped over your shoulders and tied in a knot – tennis! Umbro shorts – soccer! Shiny polyester tracksuit – hmmm, tricky … could be track and field, swimming, or Russian gangster!" None of them thought this guessing game was as humorous as I did.

But it's not just college athletes and coaches who are notorious for interesting interviews and press conferences. Sometimes it's the pros. One of my favorites is one of the most famous of all time. In 2002 NBA superstar Alan Iverson was criticized for missing a practice when he went on a legendary rant. "We talking about practice? Practice? Not a game. Practice. We talking about practice?" He said the word practice 22 times, and to this day, I can't hear the word *practice* without busting out my Iverson impression.

My last advice for you to develop a mindset conducive to success as a public speaker is that **you will need to practice**. We, indeed, are talking about practice.

People often tell me how bad they are as a speaker. "I'm just not good at it," or "It's not my personality," or "I wish I were better at public speaking." My favorite excuse was a business leader who said, "I wish I was blessed with public speaking abilities like you were, Jeff." No one has ever been "blessed" with public speaking abilities.

When someone tells me something like that, I ask them, "How often do you practice?"

"Huh?" they say.

I repeat, "How often do you practice public speaking in front of an audience?"

"Ahhhhh," they respond, "once or twice a year."

No wonder they're bad at public speaking. Doing something once or twice a year isn't frequently enough to get good at it. Imagine if you drove a car once or twice a year. Or you interviewed someone for your business once or twice a year. Or you crocheted once or twice a year. You wouldn't ever get any better. And that's ok. The strange thing about public speaking is that it's the one difficult activity people expect to be good at after only a few tries. What a bizarre expectation!

For example, golf is one of the many challenging activities I'm not good at. But I'm not upset about it or embarrassed about it. I've played golf seven times my entire life; the last time was over ten years ago. That is not enough to be good or even ok. I'm worse at golf than you are at public speaking, that's for sure! I usually start with a dozen balls; if a ball goes in the woods, I leave it there. If I run out of balls before I get through 18 holes, I go home. How insane would it be to blame the game of golf for my lack of ability or claim that I don't have the personality for golf?

Suppose I wanted to get good at golf. In that case, I'd have to play a LOT more often, work to understand the game, learn winning strategy, study great golfers, take some lessons, watch and analyze videos of myself swinging, and probably hire a personal swing coach.

Public speaking is the same. You won't magically become an effective speaker, so you can quit wishing. It takes *practice*.

I've spent a lifetime studying communication, but I would say my ability primarily comes from having gotten up and spoken in front of an audience more than 10,000 times. I've spoken to groups ranging from two or three to thousands in auditoriums, restaurants, hotels, classrooms, living rooms, banquet rooms, conference rooms, stadiums, churches, locker rooms, theme parks, libraries, factories, banks, boats, businesses, backyards, basements, and botanical gardens!

To improve, you won't have to do this as often as I do because this is my profession. But you are going to have to do more than you do now. So, I recommend you start seeking opportunities to speak in front of audiences. Ask your local Rotary or Kiwanis clubs if they ever look for speakers. Ask your pastor, priest, or rabbi if you can get up and share your testimony. Ask your supervisor or business upline if you can share at the next team meeting. See if your local school district ever looks for people with a positive message to share.

When I started my corporate speaking career (while still teaching), I asked the guy who owned the small company where my wife worked if they were interested in free training on teamwork and execution. It wasn't great, but they loved it (or just told me they loved it), and I got some experience.

For a time, I was doing a lot of speaking for universities. They said they didn't have money in their budgets to pay me, so I'd offer to do it for a coffee mug and an endorsement. University of Notre Dame, University of Michigan, Bowling Green State, Ohio State, Ohio University, etc. To this day, you can find their endorsements on my website and their coffee mugs in my kitchen cupboard!

You must work on it to learn to speak with power, effectiveness, and authenticity. It's not automatic, but it's possible. Like many things, it's simple, but it's not easy.

So now that you understand the *mindset* required to become a great speaker, we'll dig into the *skill sets* you need to develop.

CHAPTER 6

ORGANIZING YOUR PRESENTATION

The first *skill* I will challenge you to work on is organizing your presentation. This is simply deciding which ideas you plan on covering and in what order you want to cover them. In Chapter 4, I recommended a process for thinking through what you want to say to have maximum impact on the audience. Now it's time to arrange those ideas into an outline.

There are lots of general formats you can choose from. You may want to use a problem/solution structure where you address problematic issues and recommend ways to fix them. You may want to use a two-sided approach, sharing the pros and cons of a topic, or both sides of an issue, before sharing your conclusions and recommendations. You could take a chronological approach, where you talk about what happened in the past, what is happening now, and what will or should happen if people do or don't take some action. There is no right or wrong organizational strategy; think it through and make sure it makes logical sense for your topic and what you want to accomplish.

Next, I recommend that you write an outline. Depending on the time you have been given to speak, you should have two or three main points, each with two or three subpoints and an introduction, conclusion, and transitions. That's it. Keep it simple. Here's the format I recommend:

Introduction (ending in a Preview)
I.   First main point
    a.   First sub-point
    b.   Second sub-point
    c.   Third sub-point
Transition to the next main point
II.   Second main point
    a.   First sub-point
    b.   Second sub-point
Conclusion (Starting with a Review)

It is easiest to determine your main points and sub-points first, then add your introduction and conclusion, and then finish by deciding how to transition from one point to the next. (That's precisely what I'm doing as I write this book, by the way).

Let's run down the purpose of these outline elements:

INTRODUCTION

This is where you will make your first impression on the people in the audience, and as you know, you don't get a second chance at that. Hopefully, someone will introduce you and tells the audience about your background, qualifications, credibility on the topic, and why you were asked to speak at that event. If they do, you can jump right into grabbing the audience's attention. If no one introduces you, you must introduce yourself. Run briefly through your credentials and then get rolling.

It's important to thank the local leader(s) or event organizer(s) for inviting you to speak at that event. It's an opportunity to be a blessing by complimenting those leaders in front of their teams. A good leader never brags about themselves, but I love to use my credibility as a speaker to praise and compliment them in a way they can't for themselves. When the metaphorical "spotlight" shines on me, I like to reflect it to shine on others. It's kind, but it's also what I'd appreciate if I invited someone to speak to my team. And it increases the chance of me getting invited back to speak again!

You should think of some way to capture the audience's attention. It doesn't need to be a gimmick like having entrance music like a relief pitcher or starting your talk while walking up from the back of the room. Don't be weird. Keep it simple. Some possible options include telling a quick story, using a quotation, sharing a surprising statistic, asking your audience to write something down, making a prediction, or referencing a current issue in the news. Something that gets their attention and gets the ball rolling.

Next, you want to introduce the topic you'll focus on, why it's important to you, and why it should be important to the audience. The end of your introduction should *always* be a **preview**, where you share what main points you will cover.

There's an old rule of thumb in public speaking that you've probably heard. When giving a presentation:

1) Tell 'em what you're going to tell 'em

2) Then tell 'em

3) Then tell 'em what you told 'em!

FIRST MAIN POINT

When preparing a talk, I look at each main point as a mini-presentation. So, for a 15-minute talk, I'm preparing several three- to six-minute talks and then piecing them together. When you finish your first main point, it's time to transition.

TRANSITION

A transition statement is just a sentence letting the audience know you are moving from one part of your outline to another. I like to be so obvious about my structure that the audience can almost picture it in their mind. I certainly want anyone taking notes to be able to follow along easily. I will cover delivery and movement in Chapter 9, but it's worth noting that a transition is a perfect time for you to move a few steps to one side or the other. It provides a nice visual cue, as you are literally moving on to another point.

NEXT MAIN POINT

Continue making your arguments, sharing examples, or telling stories. Ensure you are making a point or leading up to making your point!

CONCLUSION

Your conclusion should start with a summary of your main points. This is the "tell 'em what you told 'em" part. Then wrap it up! One of the best ways to do that is to refer back to the story, statistic, question, or news story you started with in your introduction.

Don't forget to be very clear about what you are asking or recommending people to do when you're done talking. Have a call to action. This is your last chance to make an impression and the thing the audience will most likely remember, so make it count!

That's it! A simple, repeatable structure that you can use over and over until it's second nature. Having a blueprint like this should take much of the anxiety out of planning your presentation and boost your confidence that you will look prepared and credible.

Finally, I must give you a word of caution. Avoid *the worst ending to a presentation*, which is, unfortunately, *precisely how most people end their presentations!* This terrible idea will set you up to crash and burn; tragically, I've witnessed it happen thousands of times.

THE WORST ENDING TO A PRESENTATION

I see this happen over and over, and I cringe every time. The worst ending to a presentation is when the speaker is finished; they ask four dreaded words: "*Are there any questions?*"

WARNING – DON'T DO THAT.

54

When you end your talk by asking if there are any questions, there are only three possible things that can happen, and none of them are good:

1) ***Someone, or several people, asks a good, thoughtful, relevant question.*** This is the best possible bad scenario. Because the speaker answers the question and then asks, "Are there any other questions? . . . No? . . . No other questions . . .?" . . . (looks around) . . . (awkward silence) . . . "Ok," they say, "I guess I'm done." Then they awkwardly walk off the stage or away from the podium. What a weak ending! You're taking the most critical part of your talk and putting it into someone else's hands! And your talk fizzles out instead of ending with a bang! But it could be worse . . .

2) ***Someone, or several people, asks a dumb, rude, or irrelevant question.*** Maybe you've heard the common phrase, "There's no such thing as a stupid question." Whoever said that hadn't heard very many questions! I've seen a speaker's entire presentation derailed and taken in an entirely different direction by an enthusiastic, inappropriate, or clueless question-asker. It might be innocent, but it might be malicious. Someone with their own agenda may be looking to sabotage your agenda and hijack your presentation. I've seen it turn into a heated argument! It starts with, "Yeah, but . . ." Oh boy. And now, guess what your audience will remember about your talk? Not what you want them to, that's for sure. But it can still be worse . . .

3) ***No one has a question.*** You ask, "Are there any questions?" and everyone sits there. Silence. Crickets. It invokes Ben Stein taking attendance in *Ferris Bueller's Day Off* – "Bueller? . . . Bueller? . . ."

You wonder, "Was I just incredibly thorough? Or was nobody paying attention? Or does nobody care?" That's the weakest of all possible endings to your presentation.

If you feel you *must* ask the audience if they have any questions (and if you are giving an informative presentation, it may be appropriate), ask if anyone has a question *after* your last main point and *before* your conclusion. That way, whether people have questions or not, you still get to move to your powerful wrap-up with a solid call to action. Don't let the audience decide how you will end your presentation.

I usually say, "If anyone has any questions, I'll stay around for a few minutes after the meeting, and you can ask me then." If it's a negative troublemaker, I'd rather handle that privately without giving them my platform.

So that's how you organize a talk. Work on developing this skill; you'll kill it at future speaking events.

Any questions?

I'm just kidding! I would never end a chapter that way! But I will end with a transition. The next chapter is about a *powerful skill* you need to learn that has become my bread and butter.

CHAPTER 7

THE POWER OF STORIES

The most powerful skill I utilize in my training is my ability to tell stories. It's the cornerstone of everything I do. It's how I think, how I teach, how I inspire, how I mentor people, and it's how I parent. I'm not very good with numbers or details, but I've learned how to take even the most mundane story and tell it in a way that connects with and helps people. Honestly, it's the one thing that I am really good at. You must learn to tell stories to become a more effective, powerful public speaker.

Human beings are storytellers. Long before written language existed, humans communicated by telling stories. History and knowledge were passed down from generation to generation, as were advice, experience, and wisdom. Storytelling is one of the first language skills children develop throughout history and every culture.

We are hardwired for stories. We love to hear about the battle of good versus evil, unlikely heroes, and exciting adventures. Stories stir up emotion in a way that statistics just can't. Stories give meaning to principles and standards; they are how we make sense of the world around us. The hours and days of our lives unfold like scenes in a movie, filled with victories, disappointments, regrets, heroes and villains. And stories are an incredibly effective way to teach a lesson.

WWJD?

No matter your spiritual beliefs or religious affiliation, most people would agree that Jesus of Nazareth was one of the most influential teachers who ever lived. He taught his followers some radical lessons over 2,000 years ago, which are still around today. His teachings have been studied more than any teacher or speaker. And how did he teach? By asking questions and *telling stories*.

I'm convinced that he must have driven his apostles a little crazy. They'd ask him a question, and his replies were always something like "A farmer went out in his field . . . ," "A man had two sons . . . ," "A traveler was robbed and beaten . . . " Sometimes they got the message right away, but sometimes had to think about it a while. Those stories have endured and are still impacting people today.

While I don't think you or I will likely achieve Jesus-level storytelling and influence, it demonstrates the power and wisdom of using stories to impact others.

THE NARRATIVE PARADIGM

What I remember most from graduate school was learning about the *Narrative Paradigm*, a Speech Communication theory conceptualized by communication scholar Walter Fisher.

Since the days of Aristotle, it was generally accepted that people made decisions based on logic and reasoning, and the best way to persuade people was to make *arguments*. Fisher came along and pointed out that isn't true at all. People make decisions based on **the stories they hear**. The Narrative Paradigm claims that all meaningful communication comes in the form of *storytelling* or *the reporting of events*. For stories to influence and move people effectively, they must demonstrate *coherence* (does it make sense?) and *fidelity* (is it believable?). My experience has been that the stories that accomplish this the most effectively are *personal*.

USING PERSONAL STORIES TO CONNECT WITH AND INSPIRE THE AUDIENCE

When a speaker shares a personal story, people in the audience can instantly connect with them because it's easy to imagine being in the speaker's shoes. The most compelling stories you can tell involve a time when you were struggling, stuck, or in crisis, and you figured something out, took action in a new direction, and had a breakthrough or victory. There are certainly people in the audience who are currently stuck in a similar situation, and your story gives them the thing they need most – **hope**.

Hope is the belief that things can and will get better. It's the belief that your future will be better than your past and that you have an essential role in making it happen. Hope reduces stress, increases happiness, reduces feelings of helplessness, and improves quality of life. Hope makes people feel better, sleep better, improves relationships, facilitates patience, and sets people free! Telling your story in a way that helps others feel hope is one of the most beautiful things one person can do for another!

There is an art, though, to tell your stories *in a way that moves people*. I once spoke at an event, sharing with a team of independent business owners. I told a series of true stories about the hilarious and embarrassing adventures I've had since I started my own business – mistakes I've made, bad decisions, strange people I've met, lessons I've learned, and victories I've experienced. The audience was laughing, crying, and high-fiving. They were howling one minute and silent the next as I took them on a roller coaster journey of my ups and downs chasing my dreams. After I was done, people stayed for hours, waiting in line to talk to me, thank me, and share how many parts of their story mirrored my own. It was a fantastic night, and I was humbled and thankful for another opportunity to make a difference.

After the last person had left, one of the leaders drove me back to my hotel. It was late at night, but this successful businessman asked me if I would sit with him in the hotel lobby for a few minutes so he could pick my brain about effective communication. I was honored, to be honest, and happy to help. We grabbed a table in the empty lobby, and he said,
"I've tried to be a powerful speaker, Jeff, but I'm just not. I get that stories are the key, but my stories are terrible. People are on the edge of their seats when *you* tell stories, hanging on every word. When *I* tell stories, people look at their watches and doze off. I don't get what I'm doing wrong."

He was understandably discouraged. I had heard him speak at conferences before, and he was right. He was doing the right thing but in an ineffective way.

"I've heard you tell stories," I told him, "And they're not great. You're doing it all wrong. When **you** tell a story, here's what you share – This was the situation, this is what I did, and these were the results."

"What else is there?" he asked, exasperated.

"***You're leaving out the most important part***," I told him. He had no idea what I was talking about, and you might not, either.

"Here's how **I** tell a story," I told him. "This was the situation, ***and here's how that made me feel***, so this is what I did, ***and here's how that made me feel***, and these were the results, ***and here's how that made me feel***."

It's the ***emotional*** part that people connect with. No one has ever been in my exact same situation because everyone's life is different. But everyone has ***felt*** embarrassed, frustrated, discouraged, resolved, foolish, ashamed, proud, courageous, or victorious! When you share how events and actions in your story ***made you feel***, people are drawn in; they relate to you because they've felt that same way and are inspired to step out boldly on their own adventurous journey.

I suspect you've never read that advice before. I've read dozens of books on communication and have never seen someone explain that. I learned the hard way by observing people's reactions when a good storyteller speaks vs. how they react while others speak. That one lesson is worth way more than what you paid for this book!

If you want to see examples of me telling stories that connect with and inspire people, head to my YouTube channel, *An Epic Life*. It's impossible to show you how to do it in writing, but you can watch and listen on YouTube. Videos like "The Networking Nightmare," "The Greatest Shot of All Time," and "The Most Amazing Thing I've Ever Been a Part Of" demonstrate how I tell stories that connect with people and inspire them.

Some of the best stories are funny, but you must tread carefully. The next chapter will focus on effectively using ***humor*** in your speaking.

CHAPTER 8

USING HUMOR

As I mentioned in Chapter 3, humor can be a great way to connect with the audience and keep your presentation interesting and enjoyable. Over the years, I have experimented with many different types of humor and learned what works for me to get the audience laughing and what falls flat. I've kept the effective bits and dropped the duds. You probably don't have decades to work on this, so you must be wise and strategic. Also, I usually come into an event with high credibility, as the keynote speaker at a conference, for example, so people cut me a little more slack than you're going to get speaking in front of your co-workers or giving the toast at your brother's wedding.

Even with all my experience, sometimes I say something I think is funny, and it bombs. *Badly.* The worst one happened when I spoke to an audience of prospective business owners about the benefits and advantages of being in business for yourself (something I highly recommend if it's an option in your industry). I was talking about how anyone can and should chase their dreams, no matter how old they are. Then I said this:

"Here's an inspirational story. My grandmother is 85 years old and just entered medical school!"

After the audience said a collective "wow," with even a little applause and respectful head-nodding, I added:

"Of course . . . she's a cadaver."

Ok. That's funny. Hilarious, in my opinion! But the audience didn't agree. As soon as I said the punchline, the twelve people in the front row were all simultaneously blown back in their chairs. I mean, physically knocked back like they'd been hit with a shockwave. Their spirits were literally trying to distance themselves from me and my attempt at humor. The entire audience let out a collective "uhhhhhhh." I don't mean a groan, like when someone tells a corny joke. It sounded like someone had punched them all in the gut, and they had the wind knocked out of them! This reaction so surprised me that I started cracking up. I couldn't stop laughing uproariously at myself for doing something so wholly inappropriate at a professional business meeting. But the audience didn't know why I was laughing. I'm sure I looked more than a little unhinged.

So, I never told that joke to an audience again, even though I maintain – *that's a funny joke.*

That's the challenge with humor. Everyone thinks different things are funny. I think some movies are funny that my friends think are terrible, and vice versa. I've had one audience think something is hilarious, and the next day, another group sits there stone-faced. So, when attempting to use humor, you roll the dice every time.

The other risk with humor is that it often ends up being at someone else's expense, either someone in the room or a stereotyped group of people. That hurts people's feelings and diminishes your credibility as a speaker. It can sometimes even be considered bullying. It divides the audience by getting some people to laugh *at* others instead of everyone laughing *with* each other at something funny. When someone goes to a comedy club, they know they risk getting made fun of by the comedian on stage and accept the risk. No one came to *your* presentation to get insulted.

So how do you use humor without risking offending or insulting someone? I recommend making fun of yourself!

I use a lot of self-deprecating humor when I speak. There is an art to it, but I find it's a great way to connect with the audience, and it's hard for people to get offended when I make fun of myself. I'm not self-deprecating in a way that reduces my credibility on the topic I'm speaking about. You don't want people to think they are listening to a moron, but you do want people to know that you have some humility and are a normal person. One of the most attractive traits is someone who can laugh at themselves.

I usually tell two types of self-deprecating stories; foolish things I did in my past that I learned a lesson from, or silly mistakes I make on an everyday basis, like getting lost on the way to the venue, getting locked out of my hotel room in my swimsuit, or forgetting to pack something important for my trip. Hopefully, people are laughing with me, not at me, but either way, they find it endearing and relate to me.

Whenever I do something embarrassing – something that most people try to hide from everyone – I do the opposite. I think, "Well, this will be a funny story at my next event." My YouTube channel is full of stories of mistakes and embarrassing situations I found myself in and the lessons I learned from them, like "The Time I Found Myself in a Greek Prison" and "Getting Your Vehicle Stolen in the Dumbest Way Possible." These are true stories, I assure you, and the more embarrassing the situation, the more entertaining the story!

People **see themselves** in stories like that. After one of my speaking events last year in Upstate New York, a female Muslim doctor from Pakistan came up to talk to me. She smiled, laughed, and said, "Jeff, you and I are the same!" She continued, "I do and say the dumbest things sometimes. My family and staff always laugh about how someone so smart can be so silly sometimes!" She told me how much she learned during my session and was looking forward to applying the things I talked about so she could have less stress in her life and more productivity at work.

The fantastic thing about that story is that, **in many ways**, I have **very little** in common with that woman. Different genders, professions, educations, religions, first languages, skin colors, accents, birthplaces, etc. **And yet**, she felt that **she was just like me**. And in many ways that matter, she **IS** just like me. My spirit connected with her spirit, and I was able to help her. That's the power of humorous stories.

Since *how* you say your ideas are just as important as what you say, next is some advice for your **verbal and non-verbal delivery**.

CHAPTER 9

DELIVERING YOUR TALK

We've covered some fundamental aspects of effective public speaking, like developing a proper mindset, organizing your talk, telling stories, and using humor. But if your presentation's verbal and non-verbal delivery is weak, none of that will matter.

DON'T GIVE A SPEECH

You may have noticed that I don't usually use the terminology "giving a speech" when giving you advice about public speaking. In modern times, a "speech" usually refers to a formal presentation written word-for-word (usually by someone different than the speaker) and then read using a manuscript or teleprompter. This is the least dynamic and most boring option possible. Unless you are running for political office or reading your company's attorney-approved public press statement, *do not* read a speech to your audience. It would almost certainly be better to not speak at all than read a speech to an audience. I'd rather get punched in the face than listen to someone read a speech.

Nor should you write out a speech, memorize it, and try to recite it. This always goes poorly, and you'll get nervous and forget what you want to say. A recited speech has a meager chance of sounding spontaneous, natural, or interesting to an audience.

What works best is to prepare some notes with bullet points of the main points and anything you want to ensure you don't forget or want to get exactly right, like statistics or quoting someone. You're not "winging it" because you've researched, prepared a detailed outline, and have a plan, but you want to talk **extemporaneously**. That means, within the framework of your organized outline, you are coming up with the actual words and phrases as you go. It requires you to stay in the moment and think on your feet, but it sets you up to give a much more effective and impactful presentation.

The only exception to this advice is your introduction and conclusion. After watching thousands of college students give tens of thousands of presentations, I observed that the times they were most likely to run into trouble remembering what they wanted to say was at the very beginning or the very end. Unfortunately, those are two of the most critical parts of your talk, where you capture attention and then call for action. So, it's perfectly acceptable and even wise to think through exactly what you want to say to start your talk and what you want to say to conclude your talk, and either write it verbatim in your notes or memorize it. If you choose to do that, keep it short for your benefit!

THINK ABOUT HOW YOU LOOK

Attire. It's worth putting a little thought into how you want to dress. I like to dress a little sharper than I expect people in the audience to be dressed. If I think they will wear jeans and T-shirts, I will wear dress pants and a dress shirt. I will wear a sports coat if the audience is business casual. If I think the men in the audience will wear sports coats, I will wear a suit and tie. If I suspect they'll wear suits and ties, I wear a suit and tie with cuff links and a pocket square. You get the idea. Wear whatever you want, but you'd rather be overdressed than underdressed if you are presenting because your appearance is a big part of first impressions, and it impacts perceived credibility.

Distractions. Ditch anything on your person that could get in the way of an effective presentation. Don't chew gum or hold a pen. Empty your pockets of anything that might rattle or jingle in your pocket. I watched one nervous speaker who stuck his hand in his pocket and nervously played with a pocket full of coins for his entire presentation. It sounded like sleigh bells at Christmastime and was highly distracting.

Podiums. If possible, don't stand behind a podium the whole time. Some nervous speakers tell me they like to stand behind the podium because it gives them a sense of security and feels like a shield. Unfortunately, intentionally introducing a barrier between you and the audience isn't the best way to connect with them, and hiding never projects confidence and power.

Movement. You want to move around a little. Don't pace or wander, but intentional movement when transitioning or making a point provides some visual variety and helps keep people's attention.

Gestures. Use gestures as you speak to add emphasis to your ideas. Don't wave your arms around; just be yourself and use your hands when speaking to an audience like conversing with friends.

THINK ABOUT HOW YOU SOUND

Paralanguage refers to the nonverbal elements of speech, such as vocal tone or pitch, volume, inflection, and speaking tempo, that can convey emotion, communicate attitudes, or modify meaning. Here are a few pointers:

Volume and Inflection. Speak up and speak clearly. You don't need to shout, but speaking quietly or mumbling will tank your presentation. Shoot for a well-projected, assertive voice. If you think you'll be using a microphone, you need to practice with it. Most inexperienced speakers hold it too far away from their mouth or gesture with the hand holding the microphone, so their voice gets quieter and louder. For sure, test the microphone before the meeting starts. I travel with AA, AAA, and 9-Volt backup batteries for wireless microphones, just in case.

Rate of Speaking or Tempo. Some people speak too slowly, but much more often, people talk too fast. The problem is something called "the thought-speech differential." Your brain can process around 800 words per minute, but most people speak at about 125 words a minute. Your mind is racing faster than your mouth, which makes you want to speak faster and faster to catch up. So, you have to slow down your thinking and purposefully focus on speaking at a rate where people can hear and comprehend what you're saying. You may want to slow down even more for emphasis when making an essential point in your talk.

Tone/Pitch. At all costs, you want to avoid sounding monotone. That's the worst. Try to vary your tone and pitch to enhance meaning and hold attention.

The key to all these paralanguage elements is ***variety***. Think of it like riding a roller coaster. I've ridden hundreds of them, and the best ones provide a variety of speeds, g-forces, turns, and inversions. Some interact uniquely with the terrain or include water, fog, or fire elements. Like in an excellent presentation, the more variety, the more fun the ride is for everyone!

If you think these delivery elements don't matter as much as your words, you should know that many experts believe they are ***more*** critical. Based on years of research, professor and psychologist Albert Mehrabian developed a formula to explain a person's effectiveness and influence during face-to-face communication called the "7-38-55% Communication Rule":

7% of your influence comes from the words you say,

38% comes from your tone of voice, and

55% is what your body is doing while you are saying it.

If you sincerely want to improve your delivery, I strongly recommend ***video recording yourself*** speaking to an audience. I say that knowing that you probably won't because no one (including me) likes to watch and listen to themselves speaking on video, but if you are serious about improvement, nothing will help you more.

The last chapter in this Public Speaking section provides advice on ***effectively using visual aids like PowerPoint.***

CHAPTER 10

EFFECTIVELY UTILIZING VISUAL AIDS

Visual aids can be a helpful way to inform and persuade people and add some visual variety to your presentation to help hold the audience's attention. But you need to ensure they aren't doing the exact opposite and taking away from what you are trying to accomplish.

For example, I *never* introduce anything to the audience that distracts their focus and attention. I never pass anything around the room while I am speaking. Not a product sample, not an attendance sign-in sheet, nothing. When you do that, you are purposefully creating a situation where at least three people aren't listening to you at any given moment: The person who just had it, the person who has it now, and the person waiting to get it next! If there is some crucial element of your presentation that people need to touch and examine up close, take a break from what you are saying and have them all look, or come up to a display table, all at the same time.

I don't let other people introduce distractions while I speak, either. Sometimes a manager will want to pass a sign-in sheet around the room while I talk. I have no problem saying, "I'd rather that not be going around distracting people while I'm speaking, thank you. People can sign in during a break or during someone else's presentation."

Working with sales organizations in the food industry, I have watched dozens of times as a trainer who had prepared samples or recipes passed them around the room for people to taste while they were up front talking about the product's features, benefits, and selling strategies. It's one of the more ineffective things I've ever seen people do, but it happens regularly. When you do that, people are paying attention to either you *OR* what's being passed around at any moment. Not both. It's shooting yourself in the foot.

The most common visual aids used today are technology-based, projected visual aids like PowerPoint or Keynote. I use PowerPoint almost every time I speak somewhere, as it provides helpful visual variety and clarity. It also helps keep me on track with what I want to discuss next, so I don't need notes when I use PowerPoint.

Visual information is processed differently by the brain than spoken communication, so PowerPoint increases the chances of people understanding and remembering what you are presenting.

But I see PowerPoint used poorly *way* more often than I see it used effectively. I think we've all sat through someone reading a PowerPoint presentation to the audience, like story time in preschool, or someone who put a spreadsheet in their PowerPoint with 500 tiny, unreadable cells. It's painful to watch.

So here is some advice to ensure your digital visual aids are helping and not hurting.

MAKING YOUR POINT WITH POWERPOINT

Decide What You're Making. PowerPoint is a handy tool. If you're old enough (like I am) to have used visual aids made of posterboard, propped up on an easel, or an overhead projector, you appreciate the ease of making and using a PowerPoint file! But the very first thing you need to decide when you start to create on PowerPoint is:

Are you creating a document that people are going to read? Or are you making a visual aid to accompany and enhance a verbal presentation?

Those are two completely different projects! I've used PowerPoint to create a document, like an educational workbook or an informational file that would be emailed to people. Those documents must be comprehensive, full of detailed information, and make complete sense as a stand-alone document. But if you are making a visual aid, it needs to look and function oppositely!

When speaking, my PowerPoint slides might only include a picture, a few words, or a simple diagram. If you saw them independently of what I was saying while the slides were being shown, they wouldn't make any sense.

I often get conference organizers who ask me to "send my presentation" to them before the conference. I tell them I plan on doing an oral presentation at their event, so it can't be sent anywhere beforehand. Confused, they say, "I mean your PowerPoint." "Ooooh," I reply, "You want me to send my *visual aids*? Well, they won't make any sense by themselves." Worse yet is when someone wants to print my slides and hand them out to people beforehand. They are useless for that because that's not what they're designed to do. My slides' only value comes when they are revealed to the audience when I intend to utilize them to help me make a particular point.

In her book *How to Wow*, Frances Cole Jones said, "PowerPoint gets a bad rap when we forget it's there to *enhance* our presentation, not be our presentation. You are always the presentation, not your visuals."

Keep Your Slides Clean and Simple. We've all seen someone put a spreadsheet with hundreds of small cells embedded in a PowerPoint slide on the screen. They always say the same thing: "Sorry, this is a bit of an eye chart." They might as well say, "Sorry, I'm wasting your time with details no one can read. I'm purposely trying to give a bad presentation."

If you are making a document for people to read, it's ok to add "fine print" like a legal document. A visual aid slide that includes fine print that the audience can't read will make them understandably skeptical of you and your message.

Don't Get Carried Away. I'd recommend going easy on the fonts and animations and swooshing sounds. (If your animations include the applause sound effect, I'm leaving the room). Go for professional and utilitarian. It should enhance your points, not be the part of the presentation people remember.

Double Check and Test the Equipment. A lot can go wrong when you are connecting and projecting to use PowerPoint, and all it takes is an incompatible laptop, a bad cable, or a missing adapter to throw a wrench into your plans. For me, the most common last-minute problem is that the people organizing and setting up the meeting forgot to arrange for there even to be a projector in the room. After that happened to me a few times, I now travel with a thin backup projector and every cable, adapter, and dongle I could possibly need to connect my laptop to my client's system.

Whether using a projector and screen, a SmartBoard interactive display, or a Smart TV, test it before your event to ensure it does what you need. I bring my handheld remote for advancing slides, too. Don't assume one will be there.

That's it for my advice on public speaking! There is a lot more I could have gone into, but I chose to focus on the things I think most people need to consider and work on to become a more powerful, authentic, and compelling public speaker. If you work on developing the mindset I recommend, along with the skill set we discussed, you will be well on your way to making a difference in the lives of the people in your audience!

The next part of this book will focus on another important, challenging type of communication - ***selling***.

SELLING

Everyone works in sales. Many of you work in professional sales, but **everyone is selling something**. If you're a teacher, you're selling knowledge. If you're a lawyer, you're selling someone's guilt or innocence. If you're an accountant, you're selling accurate work and sound advice. If you're married, you are *definitely* in sales, as you had to convince your spouse to sign a lifetime contract to live with you! (Some of you outdid yourselves, landing a spouse way out of your league!)

I will focus primarily on strategies and ideas to help people who need to sell as a component of their professional work. Whether you are working in corporate business-to-business or business-to-consumer sales or own a small business that requires you to sell products or services, I'm convinced the ideas in this section can help you win.

Why am I so confident that anyone can learn to sell with effectiveness? Because I did. I used to be terrible at selling. Even after years of working in full-time business-to-business sales, I struggled. I sold just enough not to get fired until I had a breakthrough. I learned some things that helped me dramatically improve in my career.

The things I learned and the changes I made are things anyone can learn and apply. The ideas I learned changed my career and life; they can do the same for you.

CHAPTER 11

MY STORY

After five years of working as a college instructor and speech coach, I decided to make a career change. Teaching and coaching was, for me, fun, easy, and comfortable, but it didn't pay nearly as much as I could make doing other things. I decided to start a new career in professional sales. "How hard could it be?" I thought. I knew I was a good presenter, and that's essentially what selling is, right? Presenting? That's honestly what I thought, and boy, was I wrong.

The first company I interviewed with was a Fortune 500 company in the food industry. I had a friend who worked there who put in a good word with his boss. They were impressed with my resume, and I have exceptional interview skills (more on that in Chapter 26).

After interviewing with the Regional Sales Manager in Cincinnati on a Thursday afternoon, they flew me to Chicago to meet with the Divisional Sales Manager the next day. On Monday, they offered me a job!

It was crazy for me to even apply for that job, and even more so for them to *give me* the job because I didn't know *anything* about the food industry, the customers I'd be selling to, or the products I'd be selling. I spent the first few weeks in "training," learning how to fill out expense reports and information about the products I now sold. My job was selling thousands of products to foodservice distributors and operators like school districts, restaurant chains, hospitals, factories with cafeterias, and colleges. Then I learned that buying decisions were often complicated, involving RFPs, bids, sales spiffs, deviated pricing, rebates, backhaul allowances, truckload pricing, end-of-quarter deals, USDA requirements, corporate account contracts, and a thousand other variables. It wasn't rocket science, but it was surprisingly complicated and confusing.

My training on how to sell the products was woefully inadequate, but I've since discovered that it's the same training that almost all salespeople receive. The recommended strategy is to become an expert on the products, then talk to customers about them. Sample as much as possible, compare your products' strengths to the competitors' weaknesses and discuss features, benefits, and price. This ineffective strategy is based on a bizarre corporate arrogance from which almost all companies suffer – "Our products/services are SOOOO superior to our competitors; if you just talk about them and sample them, the customer won't be able to resist buying!"

The problem was that our products weren't all that superior. (Neither are yours, by the way). Our products that were higher quality than our competitors' products were more expensive than theirs. The competitive products that were more expensive than ours were of higher quality than ours.

The other reality was that every customer had a different preference regarding packaging, case quantity, ingredients, and taste, so determining "superior" was utterly subjective.

So, I started making phone calls to schedule appointments to show and discuss my products. Most of my target customers didn't need what I was selling, the price was too high, or they had a pre-existing contract with my competitors. For the first time in my professional career, people told me "No." A lot.

I was constantly frustrated and discouraged. I occasionally made a sale, but it seemed like more luck than skill, and I lost many sales for reasons that I couldn't control. I was selling just enough not to get fired, lying in bed at night worrying that someone would uncover the truth – *I'm not good at this.*

This didn't go on for a few weeks or months – this dragged on for four long years.

I was at the end of my rope and knew I needed to make a change. I considered getting out of sales altogether, but I hate quitting.

So, I decided to do precisely **what you're doing right now**. I bought a book that I hoped would help me.

I went down to the bookstore and selected a book on selling skills. I read it and discovered a few ideas I'd never thought of and a different perspective I hadn't considered. I bought another and found more new ideas and philosophies. I started applying what I was learning and immediately got better results. So, I kept at it. That year, I read more than

50 books on selling skills. Some were better than others, but I pulled out of each book ideas and wisdom that applied to my life and career. I started having great conversations with customers and felt the adversarial buyer/seller tension disappear. I developed more confidence and pride in what I could do for my customers. I started getting referrals from customers who talked to their friends and peers about what I did for them. That year, I crushed my quota, maxed out my bonus, and was awarded the company's highest award for sales leaders. The following year, I won it again. The year after that, I won it again!

Everything changed when I opened my mind to change, got aggressive about learning new things, and had the humility and courage to try something different. *I was selling five times more with one-third of the sales calls*. My stress had vanished, and I was having so much fun!

My co-workers would ask, "How do you sell so much? You hardly do any work!"

That's when another company came along and offered to ***double*** my salary if I jumped ship, which I did. I worked there for five years before starting my own company to help others learn to win.

I will share with you the things I learned and applied that made all the difference in my sales career and the things I've learned working with thousands of professionals who felt stuck and needed a breakthrough.

The first thing I suggest you understand is ***what selling even is***.

CHAPTER 12

WHAT SELLING IS AND ISN'T

Large companies often hire me to teach selling skills to their sales organizations, and I have created an impactful curriculum entitled ***Developing ASSETS: Advanced Strategies and Skills Empowering Talented Salespeople***. "Strategies" comes first in the title because what made the most significant difference in my sales career transformation had less to do with ***skills*** and more to do with my ***mindset*** - how I thought about what I was doing, what I was trying to accomplish, and the kind of conversations I was having with customers.

If you want to improve the results you get from your sales efforts drastically, and you're looking for more sales with less effort, you first need to develop a mindset conducive to winning in sales.

Most people have a completely incorrect understanding of what sales even is. They think selling is convincing or persuading others to buy what they are trying to sell, which conjures images of slick car salespeople or telemarketing scammers. Convincing and persuading is difficult and exhausting. If you are a halfway decent person, it will leave you feeling dirty and guilty, especially if you persuade people to buy products and services they don't need. That's not even persuasion. It's manipulation. And it's not just a bad sales strategy; it's immoral.

I'm not easily offended, and I usually choose not to take offense when people say something I don't like. But the most offended I've ever felt was when someone I care about said, "Jeff could sell ice to an Eskimo!" It was intended as a compliment, but I considered it a raging insult. "Is that what he thinks I do?!" I thought. Eskimos don't need ice. What kind of horrible person would sell ice to Eskimos?

The first step to becoming a world-class salesperson is understanding what selling *is* and *isn't*. It isn't convincing, persuading, or "talking people into something." When done well, ***selling is a process of partnering with a customer to help them reach their goals or get what they want***. It's the opposite of what most people think it is! When you think about it like that and learn to talk and walk that mindset, selling is nothing to be ashamed of.

On the contrary, it's one of the kindest, most loving, and most noble things someone could do! Understanding selling in this way causes shame and hesitation to disappear, and over time it's replaced with confidence and peace. Salespeople who work to develop this type of consultative mentality exude a confidence that isn't based on their ***persuasiveness*** but on their ***trustworthiness***.

And helping customers reach their goals is 10,000 times more fun and rewarding than convincing someone to buy something they don't want or need.

When you start thinking, walking, and talking this way, you develop the ability to deliver something rare indeed – ***real value***.

CHAPTER 13

THE CORE QUESTION

At the very core of the mentality that I recommend you develop if you want to get better results in your selling efforts is a crucial question you must be able to answer:

Why should a customer do business with you instead of with one of your competitors?

If you are selling skincare products, why should someone buy from you instead of from the store? Or from another business owner?

If you're selling MRI machines to hospitals, franchises to aspiring business owners, cars to drivers, soup to restaurants, vitamins to busy moms, legal services to future defendants, or grave plots to future dead people – *Why. Should. They. Buy. From. You?*

This is not a rhetorical question, nor a question with many acceptable answers. There is one correct answer to this question.

I've asked thousands of professional salespeople this question at training workshops around the country over the years, and NONE have answered how I would.

Some say, "Because our company is more honest than our competitors." Come on. The truth is that honest and dishonest people work at every company, and the customer has no idea which one you are in the beginning.

One woman replied, "Because our company is family-owned and operated." Oh, boy. "That's not a reason to buy from you," I said, "All that means is that some of the people working here didn't earn their jobs."

"Because our prices are better!" some salespeople answer. "Even if that was a good strategy (and it's not), I doubt it's true," I reply. "Your products are priced right, just like everyone else's. If your products were too expensive, someone else would sell the same quality product for less, and you'd be out of business. If your prices were too low, your company would go bankrupt. Your products are priced just right, just like your competitors' products are." That's how free enterprise works.

No one yet has answered the Core Question the way I would:

Question: Why should a customer do business with you instead of with one of your competitors?

Answer: *Because they believe that they are more likely to reach their goals working with you than with your competitors.*

Every customer has *something* they are trying to accomplish. B2B (business-to-business) customers may be trying to grow their revenue, increase profits, decrease costs, expand to new markets, attract new clients, drive employee engagement, reduce hassles, increase customer loyalty, or any number of a thousand different things. B2C (business-to-consumer) customers may be trying to lose weight, be more productive, look younger, sleep better, reduce stress, feel safer, or enjoy their life. If they believe they are more likely to get whatever they want working with you, you both win. If not, you lose, and you should lose.

That sounds simple, but it's profoundly important and should be the focal point of all your sales efforts. Everything you do regarding that customer should be focused on finding out what they are trying to accomplish, determining whether you can help them achieve it, and showing them exactly how you can!

One of the things that helped me develop a proper mentality was thinking through ***how customers saw me and the value I brought to the table***.

CHAPTER 14

HOW DO CUSTOMERS PERCEIVE YOU?

When I started working in sales, I never thought through how customers viewed me, my approach, and my sales efforts, which was naïve and foolish. Each customer (and potential customer) perceives you differently. There is a hierarchy of value on which all salespeople exist in the mind of their customers. I first learned this concept from the book *Beyond Selling Value: A Proven Process to Avoid the Vendor Trap* by Mark Shonka and Dan Kosch.

Imagine a pyramid where the lowest level of perception is a ***vendor***. A salesperson who is perceived as a vendor adds very little value. They might be viewed as the person who takes the order or brings product samples, and their conversations with customers are about pack size, case size, and price. Thirty years ago, vendors brought *some* value because they had information in their heads, briefcase, or catalog that the customer could not know. Then a critical change occurred: the internet was invented. Today's customers have access to infinitely more information about *your* products and *your competitors'* products on a device in *their* pocket than you could possibly have in your head or briefcase. Vendors are sales dinosaurs and don't even know it because they add almost no value to the customer. Don't be a vendor.

A step up from vendor on the pyramid of customer perceptions is a *problem solver*. This is the salesperson who can address product-related issues. A problem-solver might help a diabetic client access sugar-free energy drinks or match an insurance customer with the perfect policy. The ability to utilize your portfolio of products or services to solve customers' problems is way better than being a "vendor," but it's the highest most salespeople ever get on the pyramid of customer perceptions.

There are two more levels, however. A step up from being a problem solver is to be perceived as a *business resource*. A person perceived as a business resource goes beyond features, benefits, pack size, and price and has conversations with customers about what they really *want*. They are talking about how customers can reach financial goals, increase business profitability, attract and train world-class talent, expand into new markets, grow brand awareness, drive employee engagement, execute effective marketing strategies, etc.

I once watched a trash bag salesman point out to a restaurant chain owner that their garbage cans were suffering from what he called UBO (*Unsightly Bag Overage*). The bags were too big for the cans, with a lot of plastic hanging over the can. By showing the owner the proper size to purchase for a product they used many times a day in each restaurant, he saved them a lot of money! That's being a business resource.

Few salespeople live and work at the business resource level because it requires much more than product knowledge. It requires business acumen, industry knowledge, and the willingness and skills to discover one's customers' goals. Most salespeople have never even thought about how they are perceived, so they don't know to strive for higher levels because they don't know that more elevated levels exist! So, they keep losing sales to better salespeople and making excuses for the lost business.

One level on the pyramid is higher than business resource – **Strategic Resource**. You make the leap to this level when you can shift your conversations with customers from how to help them grow their business or improve their lives **today** to how to help them grow their business or improve their lives **in the future**.

You and your customer have developed a **genuine partnership** at this highest level. You are thinking up new ways you can help them grow their business and reach their goals, and *they* are thinking up new ways they can help you grow your business and achieve your goals. It's powerful, rewarding, and fun!

Many years ago, I had lunch with another outside salesperson from our company who wanted some advice. She needed help getting appointments with the decision-makers at her target customers. I asked her what she said when she got them on the phone. She said, "I tell them who I am and ask if they would give me a few minutes of their time so I could tell them about our great products."

She honestly had no idea what a terrible approach that was. "So, you're asking busy strangers to GIVE YOU TIME – *the single most valuable thing they possess* - so you can come in and talk about what is important to you?" I asked. "No wonder you're having trouble getting appointments!"

I told her I never had trouble getting appointments because I had a very different approach based on my understanding of customer perceptions. Every situation is a little different, but after introducing myself over the phone to a potential customer, I'd say, "I have an excellent track record of helping organizations like yours grow their sales and profits, attract new customers, and build extraordinary teams. Would you be open to me coming by and discussing what you are trying to accomplish over the next five years and how I might be able to help you do it?"

Do you see how different that is? I'm **giving** instead of **taking**, focused on **them** more than **myself**, and setting the tone from the very beginning that I am interested in a long-term relationship, not just a sales transaction. I was also filtering, as I am looking for the *right kind of customer* – someone interested in partnering with a strategic resource, not someone who wants to save a few bucks on an order or is just curious about what I sell.

I hope you're starting to see how some slight shifts in your thoughts about what you're doing and why can make a big difference.

I'm sure you've heard the phrase, "The key to success isn't just working **hard**; it's working **smart**." That sounds great, but it's easier said than done because no one knows what "smart work" looks like. Everybody is already working as smart as they know how.

THIS is working smart.

The next chapter will help you work even smarter by focusing on permanently **differentiating yourself** from your competitors.

CHAPTER 15

DIFFERENTIATION

To develop the proper mindset needed for a breakthrough in your sales efforts, you must shift how you think and talk about *differentiation*. After working with thousands of professional salespeople, it's been my observation that:

99% of salespeople talk to customers about how *they* (**the salesperson**) are different from *their* competitors.

The best 1% of salespeople talk to customers about how *they* (**the customer**) can be different from *their* competitors.

That is a significant distinction. One of those topics is of *zero* interest to your customers, and the other is of urgent, complete interest to your customers! When I realized this and shifted the kind of conversations I had with clients, my sales doubled overnight.

When I speak about this to live audiences, I ask them if anyone can tell me the difference between two and four. People shout out "two," which I tell them is incorrect. "Double?" "Square root?" Nope. Occasionally, someone will think outside the box and say, "A 2 is made out of a curved line, and a 4 is made out of straight lines." Creative answer, but still not what I am looking for. (Do you know?)

I finally point out that they are mistakenly assuming that I am talking about math. They thought I meant "*two and four*," but what I meant was "*to and for*." My question isn't about **numbers**; it's about **prepositions**:

When an ordinary salesperson shows up, something is happening **TO** the customer. When a great salesperson shows up, something is happening **FOR** the customer.

The difference between "to" and "for" is between being a vendor and a strategic resource. It's the difference between pestering customers and delivering value. It's the difference between a series of no's and making consistent, recurring sales. It's all the difference in the world.

I learned this idea when reading a book by renowned restauranter Danny Meyer, *Setting the Table: The Transforming Power of Hospitality in Business*. He uses "to" and "for" to explain the difference between **service** and **hospitality**. Service is the technical aspects of getting what you paid for promptly. Hospitality is rooted in **thoughtfulness** by connecting your brain and heart to let your customers know you are on their side. If that idea worked for five-star restaurants in New York City, it could also work for my sales efforts.

So, I started thinking strategically about what I could say and do on my sales calls to ensure the customer knew I was on their side. It wasn't a slick technique to close more sales. Those never work long-term. It was the simple realization that how the customer *feels about me*, and by extension, my company and products, is an essential part of the process. This mindset also resonated in my spirit because it aligned with my deep desire to do things with my life that made a difference in the lives of others.

That's the catch in my advice, by the way. People hear about how I dramatically increased my sales results and have helped many others do the same, and they want to know, "What's the catch?" The "catch" is that this approach only works if you are a good person, and this strategy will backfire if you are a disingenuous, manipulative, lying user. If you sincerely enjoy helping people, developing good relationships, and solving problems, learning to be a consultative strategic resource is a simple and powerful way to differentiate yourself from all the other salespeople.

This has nothing to do with your education level, product knowledge, or skills. It's simply *how you think* about who you are and what you do.

And as you differentiate yourself as a salesperson, you are fortifying that customer relationship against potential attacks from your competitors. Imagine how silly it looks when one of my competitors shows up with a coupon or a limited-time-only special price at a customer where I have established myself as a differentiated strategic partner. They don't have a chance.

I love this paragraph from the book *Blue Ocean Strategy* by Renée Mauborgne and W. Chan Kim:

"The only way to beat the competition is to stop *trying* to beat the competition. Instead, focus on making the competition irrelevant by creating a leap in value for buyers and your company, thereby opening up new and uncontested market space."

The idea of Blue Ocean Strategy is that most companies and salespeople spend all their energy fighting over the same unprofitable pieces of business. They are like sharks in bloody waters. And they hit on the magic word, suggesting you create a leap in **value.**

CHAPTER 16

DELIVERING VALUE

I challenge you to think differently about how you add value to the sales process and your customers. Usually, when companies or sales-people talk about "value-added," they are referring to products. Value-added products are obtained after one or more processing stages, with increased value compared to the initial raw material. Strawberries are turned into jam; crude oil is refined into gasoline. The chicken nuggets in your freezer are a delicious value-added product.

When I'm talking about adding value, I mean something else entirely. I'm discussing ways **YOU** can add value, not the products you sell.

Let's talk about the products you sell for a minute. I'm sure they are great.

But they're not *that* great.

When I do live training for sales organizations, I ask the crowd, "How many of your company's products are SO good - SO much better than your competitors' products - that they sell themselves?" The room gets quiet as they think about it. The eventual, obvious answer is – none of them.

That's not a bad thing, by the way. That's great news! Because if your company had products that were so good that they sold themselves, the company wouldn't need salespeople.

There was a time, many years ago, when an innovative company would release a product or service that was vastly superior to anything else on the market. It would take years for competitors to catch up and offer similar products at a comparable price. Those days are long gone. Advancements in communication, technology, and manufacturing have sped up that process. Now every company has competitors for every product and service. There will always be tiers of quality and price, but the days of unique one-of-a-kind products are gone. There is a wide array of cars on the market, for example. Some are of higher quality than others, and those have higher prices. But every car, at every price tier, has competitors from other companies at similar prices. Same with french fries, protein bars, furniture, shampoo, medical equipment, energy drinks, pharmaceuticals, and sporting goods. More and more products have become commodities.

This is excellent news if you work in sales. As products and services become more commoditized, the role of a skilled sales professional becomes more crucial. There has never been a better time for you to grow your business or sales career!

I'm challenging you to think about ways to add value for your customers *outside the product*. You have one advantage that your competitors will never have – *you*! What skills do you bring to the table? What relevant expertise can you offer? If nothing else, you bring *perspective* to your customers because you know the challenges your other customers face and the strategies they use to win. I guarantee you have abilities and valuable knowledge going unused and unleveraged.

Here's the question I recommend you ask yourself:

What can I do for my customers that my competitors can't or won't do?

If you can develop a relevant, valuable answer to that question, guess what? *You don't have competitors anymore!*

My answer to that question was primarily my public speaking skills. I knew I possessed a skill that my competitors probably didn't. So, I started asking my customers and future customers (restaurant chains, school districts, distributors, universities, hospitals, stadiums, factories, etc.) if they would be interested in having me provide training for their employees, franchisees, or customers. When asked how much I would charge, I'd say, "I won't charge anything! We're partners. I will do everything I can to help you grow your business and reach your goals. I expect you to do everything you can to help my business grow and reach my goals."

People ask me, "Do you really talk to your customers like that?" Yep. And they appreciate it.

So, I provided training at no cost to them. (Not "free," by the way. Never "free." Nothing is free). I spoke to groups of franchise owners about customer service and attitude, school district employees about teamwork and handling change, and healthcare groups about talent acquisition and stress management. My favorite was speaking to distributor sales organizations about *advanced selling skills* while I was modeling for them *advanced selling skills!*

The more value I brought to my customers, the more of my products they bought. Many started looking for excuses to buy more and more. They owed me and wanted to help my company like I had helped theirs. And I left my former competitors in the dust because the salespeople at those companies ***couldn't do*** or ***wouldn't do*** what I was doing for my customers.

Like William McEwen says in his book *Married to the Brand*, "Anything that is difficult for your rivals to duplicate can provide your company with the holy grail of brand building: a sustainable competitive advantage."

There is an element of negotiation skills in high-level value-adding partnerships. I was ***trading*** something ***easy for me to do*** but very ***valuable to my customer*** (speaking and training) for something ***easy for them to do*** but very ***valuable to me*** (purchasing the products I sold). In exchange for an hour or two of my time and expertise, they would buy truckloads of the products I was selling! It was a beautiful, profitable win/win.

You may think, "Well, I'm not a professional speaker." I know. My situation is unique. ***So is your situation.*** I suspect that you are great at ***something***. I hope you are! Whatever that thing is, ***give it to your customers and see what happens***. If you're not good at anything, get good at something! Become an expert in some relevant topic your customers would value.

In his excellent book *The Little Red Book of Selling*, Jeffrey Gitomer said, "If you want to build a relationship, if you want to get referrals, you have to become known as **an** expert or **the** expert in whatever you do. This requires hard work and study on your part. If you're not willing to do that, my immediate recommendation is to run down to the post office and get a nice safe job down there selling stamps at the counter."

Adding exceptional levels of value to your customers leads to ongoing sales and customer loyalty and helps you avoid the **price trap**. Consider this question:

True or False: The more **value** you bring to a customer, the less **price** matters.

The obvious and only correct answer to that question is **true**. The more value you bring, the less price matters. That is a fact. But, if that's true, so is the inverse of that statement – **If you don't bring value, all that's left is price!** I often hear salespeople using price as an excuse for losing a sale or some business they used to have. "My competitors have better prices. What am I supposed to do?" They don't like it when I point out that losing sales based on price isn't a good excuse; it's an indictment of their abilities and mindset as sales professionals.

If you consistently lose sales because of price, you must improve your ability to deliver something outside the product your customers value. It must be more than what they expect and get from other vendors. It needs to be **extra**.

CHAPTER 17

GOING THE EXTRA MILE

Since we are talking about mindset, focusing on the powerful concept of *going the extra mile* is essential. Everyone has heard the phrase so often that it's become a cliché, but it is a crucial mindset you need to develop if you are going to win in selling.

Ordinary business professionals do precisely what is expected of them. Extraordinary professionals find ways to deliver more. According to Jodie Cook, who writes about entrepreneurship for *Forbes*, "Finding novel and surprising ways to go the extra mile turns skeptics into fanatics and passive bystanders into loyal customers who tell their friends. Without their clients, businesses wouldn't exist. Safeguarding your future means putting energy into the extra mile until it's second nature."

You may not even know what "going the extra mile" means. The idea originates from a story in the Bible. Jesus was giving his most famous speech, the Sermon on the Mount. Overlooking the Sea of Galilee, He spoke to a group of listeners consisting of Jewish farmers and peasants living under the Roman government's harsh rule. That's when Jesus said something controversial and shocking:

"If anyone forces you to go one mile, go with him two miles."

He was referring to the cruel and unpopular law that allowed any Roman soldier to stop any Jewish man and force him to drop his pack and carry the soldier's belongings for one mile.

Why would Jesus say such a thing? Because ***doing more than you must*** shows ***that you are a different kind of person***. When you voluntarily choose to do more and go further than you must, it reveals that you operate from a different worldview than everyone else. It's surprising and has the power to transform others and situations.

One of the best-selling self-help authors of all time, Napoleon Hill, reportedly spent 30 years studying and interviewing the most successful people in the world. In his 1945 book *The Master-Key to Riches*, he wrote, "An important principle of success in all walks of life and all occupations is the willingness to go the extra mile, which means the rendering of more and better service than that for which one is paid, and giving it in a positive mental attitude."

So, giving more or better service than that for which one is paid. A rare thing in today's world, where most people want to be paid more than what they have earned. Entitlement has run rampant. Being willing to do more than what you are paid to do is such a simple and powerful way to differentiate yourself.

How you implement this depends on your industry, products, and customers. You could drive and hand-deliver some samples or a contract that could have been mailed or emailed. You could write a handwritten thank you note. You could offer to fly at your own expense to a meeting that could have been done virtually over the web.

The part of the quote from Napoleon Hill that resonates with me is the very end – ". . . and giving it in a positive mental attitude." Not salty or begrudging, but sincerely, because you want to. People can tell the condition of your heart, and they will detect if you really care or are just scheming with a slick technique.

The difference between ordinary and extraordinary in any endeavor is five letters – ***extra***. If you have the humility, desire, and wisdom to develop this habit, you'll find yourself in rare air regarding how your customers feel about you. ***There's never a traffic jam on the extra mile.***

When you learn to go the extra mile for your customers habitually, you will start getting rid of one thing that is certainly holding you back – ***satisfied customers.***

CHAPTER 18

THE CURSE OF SATISFIED CUSTOMERS

The last major shift in mentality I recommend is **getting rid of all your satisfied customers**. Satisfied customers are dangerous; moving the needle in your sales efforts will be hard if you have too many.

For years, I was *shooting* for satisfied customers. That's the goal, right? Then, along my journey of becoming a more effective, consultative, strategic resource, I realized I was wrongly looking at the whole idea.

The problem is that people see *"customer satisfaction" as a continuum*, with "unsatisfied" at one end and "satisfied" at the other. I'm sure you've taken hundreds of surveys in your life that looked like this:

1   Completely Dissatisfied
2   Dissatisfied

3	Neutral
4	Satisfied
5	Completely Satisfied

The problem is that "satisfied" is such a low bar. Can't we do better than that? *Satisfied*?? And what's the difference between "satisfied" and "completely satisfied," anyway? It's nonsense. When talking about a customer service experience, "satisfied" is so lame. It's lukewarm and blah.

Whenever I check out of a hotel, they ask me the same question: "Sir, was your stay satisfactory?" Guess what I almost always say? "Yep." The TV worked, the bed was ok, and the shower had hot water. *Satisfactory*. It wasn't great; I wasn't blown away. I'm in no hurry to return and will probably forget I even stayed there. I'm certainly not recommending it to my friends. It was simply **only** satisfactory.

One day, I was in Wisconsin to speak at a conference and stopped for breakfast at a national chain restaurant. After eating my mediocre omelet and average coffee served with adequate customer service, the woman at the cash register looked at me and timidly asked, "Was everything ok?"

"Yes!" I replied, "That precisely describes my experience here this morning!"

It was . . . *ok*. Average and forgettable. I hope you are aiming for something more than that with *your* customers!

There is a type of customer that is FAR more desirable than a satisfied customer. One that is so impressed with the quality of the value you bring to them that they become a *loyal customer*. Loyal customers take pride in doing business with you, and they're not tempted to cheat on you, so to speak, with other suppliers.

When you think about it, a "satisfied customer" isn't much better than a dissatisfied one. Because do you know what dissatisfied customers turn into quickly? *Former* customers. So, the satisfied customers most businesses and salespeople are proud of are the *least satisfied* customers they have!

Once, a divisional president for one of the biggest companies in America contacted me and asked to meet. He had heard from some of his peers around the country that I did powerful training that helped salespeople succeed. He was skeptical that anyone could better train and equip his salesforce than he already had. I met with him in his big office, and we had an interesting conversation:

"I have a question for you, Jeff," he said. "We survey our customers and ask them if they are satisfied with the quality of our service, and we score *very* high."

He leaned forward for emphasis and repeated, "*VERY* high."

He leaned back and continued, "And yet we lose customers to our competitors every day. How would you explain that?"

I answered, "Let me guess: When you survey your customers and ask them if they are satisfied, between 90% and 95% say they are."

Shocked, he said, "How did you know that!? Yes! 92.6% of our customers report that they are satisfied."

I didn't tell him that *every* company that surveys its customers and asks that silly question gets "yes" from between 90% and 95% of respondents! Some are so bold to brag about it: "9 out of 10 Ford owners would recommend a Ford!" "9 out of 10 Verizon customers are satisfied with their coverage and service!" Of course, they are! Because people who don't like Fords *don't buy Fords!* People who are dissatisfied with Verizon switch to another provider. All the ones left are satisfied!

But I didn't tell the division president any of that in our meeting. I said, "When you book me to speak for your team, I will explain it to everyone and teach you how to stop losing so many customers!" He did book me, and I had a great training day with his team. Their sales went way up, and he was promoted to national president of that company!

When reinventing my sales career, I stopped being ok with satisfied customers and started focusing on what I could do to make them loyal. Then I realized there was a type of customer that was way better than a loyal customer. That's one who is SO loyal, blown away, and impressed by what you do that they tell their friends and peers about you. Other authors have called these *raving fans* or *apostles*. They are so impressed with you and your abilities that they spread the good news!

Ken Blanchard wrote a book about this called *Raving Fans: A Revolutionary Approach to Customer Service*. He said, "Your customers are only satisfied because their expectations are so low and because no one else is doing better. Just having satisfied customers isn't good enough anymore. If you really want a booming business, you have to create Raving Fans."

I know this idea sounds simple, but it can change everything. When I learned this lesson, I booked appointments with all my customers to discuss it. As crazy as it sounds, this is precisely what I told them, and I recommend you say this to your customers too:

"I'm doing a new, exciting promotion. I'm getting rid of all my satisfied customers!" They'd look at me confused. "I'm getting rid of all of my satisfied customers and replacing them with blown away, amazed, can't-believe-how-much-I-help-them,   can't-wait-to-tell-their-friends customers! *What could I do differently to turn you into one of those?*"

This led to great conversations. Many said, "Well, I think you're doing great." I would reply, "Awesome, but promise me – if you ever think of something I could be doing better, any way I could better help you succeed, you'll tell me." It's still a productive conversation even if they don't ask for any changes.

Some customers said, "Since you asked, I would love it if you _____."
One asked if I could come by earlier in the morning when she was less busy. One wanted me to bring samples of products I never imagined they'd be interested in. One customer asked if I had access to trend information for his industry (which I didn't, but I could do some research). Shooting for raving fans, instead of being satisfied with satisfied customers, helped me dramatically increase my sales and further insulate myself against my competitors' attacks on my business.

This same mentality continues to drive the success of my training company now that I do more speaking and training than selling. My whole marketing strategy is creating raving fans and letting them do my marketing for me! My company has generated millions of dollars in revenue without spending a penny on advertising. The people who love the training I do tell their friends and peers, who tell their friends and peers. I hope this book adds enough value to your life that you will tell your friends about it. Just don't give them *your* book! Buy another one and give it as a gift.

Now that we've covered the proper selling **mindset** let's explore some *skills* you should consider developing. The first one is ***organizing your sales conversations***.

CHAPTER 19

ORGANIZING YOUR SALES CONVERSATIONS

When I started working in sales, I did what everyone else did. I'd show up for an appointment, engage in some small talk about the weather or the local sports team, and then talk about my products. My customers were perfectly ok with this because it's the same format they've seen many times, and it's what they expected. Plus, they wanted to hurry the process because salespeople were mainly wasting their time, showing them products or services they didn't want or need or products they had seen many times before.

I would do these calls over and over again. Sometimes with the same target customer, every three months or so, for years. The format was always the same. I'd talk about my products, how great they are, how superior they are to my competitors' products, and the features and benefits the corporate marketing department had told us to discuss.

The "customer" (I use that term loosely because they hardly ever bought anything) would shoot down my products one by one: too expensive, wrong package size, wrong ingredients, bad timing, regulation problems, whatever.

Then I'd move on to the following product. Like a bad infomercial – "But wait! There's more!" After no, no, no, no, maybe another time, no, no, no, I would thank them for their time and head to my next appointment. The whole thing was essentially a waste of everyone's time. Occasionally, I would sell something, primarily by sheer chance. I wasn't exactly executing strategy at a high level. More like Forrest Gump stumbling into success by accident.

I would tell my boss that things weren't going great. His advice was, "Be persistent! Eventually, they'll buy from you because they feel sorry for you!" Great. Pity sales. My dream career has come true.

So, when I started reading and learning and decided to change my mindset about selling, I knew I needed to change the format of these calls. I realized I needed to stop talking **about what was important to me** and start talking **about what was important to my customers**. That was an obvious result of my new, developing, strategic resource mindset. The problem was that I didn't know what was important to them, and assuming wasn't getting me far. I needed to gather some information. I couldn't just jump into talking about myself and my products anymore.

With some trial and error, I developed a structure for sales conversations that got results. I recommend that you adopt this format when talking to your customers. You might spend thirty minutes going through these steps, sometimes five minutes, or several appointments over time. How do you decide how much time to dedicate to the process? *The size of the prize*. If you're selling protein shakes or residential lawn care services, you might run through these steps in just a few minutes with a single potential client and cut to the chase sooner than later. If you're selling insurance policies or air treatment systems to a regional business chain, you may want to go deeper and spend an hour or two together. If you're selling a robotic surgical machine to a hospital for $2.3 million, you may need to slow your roll and stretch this process into several meetings over time, probably involving multiple decision-makers. But the structure of the process will be essentially the same.

Here is the structure I recommend for effective sales conversations:

1) **Rapport-building**. You don't want to spend too much time engaging in "small talk," which can get awkward fast, but some introductory conversation is essential. I like to connect with someone by finding something we have in common. If we're meeting in their office or workplace, I look around. There are usually things like pictures of family, sports memorabilia, or framed diplomas. Establishing that we are both parents, NFL fans, or love to travel builds some common ground and goes a long way toward dissipating any potential adversarial buyer/seller tension. I like to introduce the purpose of the meeting and the potential benefits of the conversation so they know what to expect.

2) **Questioning**. You *must* ask some questions before talking about what you're selling. You have to. If you don't, you are throwing darts at a dartboard with a blindfold on. It's worse than that. You

are throwing darts blindfolded in a room that might not even have a dartboard! This is the most critical step that is typically skipped over altogether. The next chapter will focus on asking questions that get the necessary information to add value.

3) **Listening**. You're not just asking questions to seem interested. You need to work on your active listening skills. If you listen to someone, you'll discover what is important to them. Listen for what they say and what they don't say. Listen to their tone to detect frustration with parts of their life or business. Listen for any pain that you might be able to help with. Take notes and ask follow-up questions. Listen for anything that surprises you or you didn't know before. Don't jump into selling immediately when you hear a single problem. Keep asking questions as long as they will let you and listen carefully. We'll get more into this skill in Chapter 20.

4) **Transition from Information-Gathering to Presenting**. After showing them the respect of letting them share with you and discovering as much as possible about them, it's time to transition into presenting your solutions. Find a simple phrase that works for you: "I think I have some idea now about the challenges you're facing and what you're trying to accomplish, and I have some ideas that can help you reach your goals." After you have sincerely listened to them, it's human nature for them to reciprocate and listen sincerely to what you have to say.

5) **Positioning**. This is where it gets fun. Once you know what your customer wants and needs, you make recommendations by positioning your products or services as solutions to their problems. Instead of trying to jam square pegs into round holes, you

recommend customized ideas and strategies. Skip your products that don't fit and focus on the ones that do. Highlight the features of the products most relevant to your customer's situation. You're brainstorming, recommending, advising, and providing ideas. This is where you are adding value to their life or business.

6) **Addressing Concerns**. This step is what many people call "handling objections." I'm not a big fan of that terminology. We'll dig into this in Chapter 24.

7) **Closing the Sale**. I'm not a fan of that term, either. Ideally, you *build* partnerships and *open* long-term relationships more than "closing" anything. This is where you go to the next step of doing business together. You either take their order, or agree to have contracts drawn up, or whatever is next in your industry. There have been many studies that show that most salespeople talk and talk about their products and then never ask for the sale! I suppose it's because they don't like the possibility of rejection. But, if you use the approach I advocate in this book, you greatly minimize the chance of rejection. When you've built rapport, asked good questions, listened sincerely, recommended solutions to their needs, and addressed their concerns – doing business together is the next natural step!

Once you know the structure you plan on executing in your sales conversations, *questioning* is the next skill you must develop.

CHAPTER 20

QUESTIONING

When I do selling skills training workshops with full-time professional salespeople, this is *always* the skill people think they have mastered, and it's always the skill they struggle most with when we break up into small groups to practice. Always. Sometimes they are shockingly bad.

I split people into pairs to practice asking open-ended questions to learn about a customer's business. One person plays the salesperson's role, and the other person plays the part of the customer and has a sheet of paper listing confidential information about that business, the customer's problems, goals, etc. – things the other person couldn't know without asking questions. The point of the exercise is to ask good questions and learn as much as they can. I walk around the room, and it is painful to see these adult learners try to ask quality, relevant, valuable questions.

It reminds me of the scene from *The Matrix* right after Neo is freed from the Matrix. He asks, "Why do my eyes hurt?" To which he is told, "Because you've never used them before."

Some salespeople I've trained could say, "Why am I so bad at asking good questions?" I'd respond, "Because you've never used questioning skills before."

I'm not the only one who's observed this. Jeffrey Gitomer, the author of *The Little Red Book of Selling*, said, "The most important aspect of making a sale is also a major weakness of every salesperson. Asking questions." ***Every*** salesperson.

Stephen Schiffman wrote an entire book about this called *Ask Questions, Get Sales*. I like this quote: "The let-me-show-you-what-we-can-do-for-you instinct is usually more than strong enough to completely over-power any instinct to find out what challenges the prospect faces in his organization."

That is so true. Your instinct is to jump in and start presenting! Start selling! It takes wisdom and discipline to ask questions first.

Until this becomes a skill and a habit, I recommend you make a list of questions *before* your meeting. There is no shame in doing that; it shows you are prepared and professional. Not some standard question-naire, but intelligent, targeted, relevant questions based on the person and business you are talking with.

What kind of questions should you prepare? Here are some guidelines:

Ask open-ended questions. Not yes-or-no queries or ones that require short, specific answers. Avoid questions like, "Are you happy with your current supplier?" Or "What kind of laundry detergent do you use?" You learn very little from closed-ended questions, and when you go back and forth with those, it gets awkward fast, and it starts feeling like an interrogation instead of a conversation.

Open-ended questions are designed to get someone talking. When people start talking about themselves or their business operation, there is no limit to what valuable information you might learn!

Examples of open-ended questions that get the customer talking are questions that start like this:

- How have you successfully used …?

- What do you find most challenging about …?

- If you could change anything around here, …?

- How do you decide . . .?

- What do you like most about …?

If you are not used to asking questions like this (and most people aren't), it's like learning a new language. But it's crucial that you learn the skill of asking open-ended questions.

Avoid leading questions. Don't ask questions like, "Would you like to be healthier?" or, "Wouldn't you love to save more money?" Of course, they would. Or, God forbid, "What if I could show you a product that was better (or less expensive) than anything you've seen? Would you buy it?" Leading questions are cheesy and insult the intelligence of the customer.

Ask questions that provide insight into what's important to the customer. You want to ask questions that get someone thinking and sharing. Whenever someone starts talking and sharing, do you know what they talk about? **What's important to them**. People who love to run will tell you about running. People who love to travel will talk about travel. Customers who hate when their vendors raise prices will tell you about that. Customers who want reliable supply chain support will talk about it.

Two of my favorite questions to ask a new or future business-to-business customer are, "Who is your favorite vendor to work with and why?" and "Who is your least favorite vendor to work with and why?" I don't care what the names of the companies are, but I *do care* about the *why*. Customers will start pouring out what they love and hate regarding salespeople, suppliers, contracts, pet peeves, the things that drive them crazy, and the path to their hearts. They will lay out a roadmap for you to turn them into a raving fan!

Ask questions designed to go beyond "needs." Norman Vincent Peale is attributed as saying that the key to success is finding a need and filling it. I've heard that my whole life and it made sense. Then, when I was reinventing myself as a sales professional, I read a book, and one sentence in that book got me thinking. The book was *Think Like Your Customer* by Bill Stinnett. The sentence that got my wheels turning was simple but profound:

"People buy what they need to get what they want."

People buy what they **need** to get what they **want**. I realized that behind every "need" was something emotional, something the customer really **wanted**. And finding out what that was could be the secret to helping me help them win.

So, a customer might need eco-friendly products, but *why they want them* is just as important, if not more so. Maybe it's their passion, and they want to save the planet. Maybe their boss is pushing this initiative on them. Perhaps they see the marketing advantages of telling *their* customers how green they are. Maybe they want to pose with the products on Instagram.

Another customer may *need* an air purifier but *wants* to breathe clean air. Or maybe they are a dentist's office or dog groomer who wants to market the clean air in their lobby to their customers.

A family might *need* a babysitter, but they *want* a peaceful night out without worrying about what is happening back home. (Parents will pay more for a quiet night out – which is priceless – than they will for "babysitting services," which is a commodity).

Knowing the *want* behind the *need* is powerful and will pay off when you get to the positioning phase of the sales conversation.

What kind of things do **your** customers want? A partial list might include more profit, less hassle, less risk, fewer headaches, a better night's sleep, more energy, greater productivity, being respected by their peers, peace of mind, engaged employees, longevity in relationships, hope for a better future, to get sick less frequently, and on and on. The closer you can come to delivering anything they truly want, the more likely you are to turn a satisfied customer into a raving fan, and the less price matters.

I once asked a customer who was a successful restaurant owner, "If you could accomplish anything huge in the next five to ten years, what would it be?"

He said, "I'd love to purchase the property next door and expand our operation to include a retail bakery and gift shop."

I followed up with, "Why would that be important to you to do?"

His answer surprised me: "My dad started this restaurant, and it was always his dream to buy that property and expand with a bakery and a gift shop. He died before he could make it happen, and I took over as owner." He got a little emotional and continued, "I think if I were able to make my dad's dream come true, he'd be proud of me."

Whoa. That's deep. And real. And awesome! I knew immediately what kind of ideas and products I would start bringing that dude. Concepts focused on helping him grow and expand that business, ideas to make his dad proud. I worked with him as a strategic resource for years, sometimes selling him products and helping him promote them on his menu, sometimes just brainstorming because two heads are better than one. When he accomplished the dream and expanded that restaurant, I was happy and proud of him, but I also got much personal satisfaction from my small contribution. And it all came from one good open-ended question.

Ask follow-up probing questions. Sometimes a customer will give an excellent answer to an open-ended question, but there is more on that topic that hasn't been said. Don't just rush to the next question on your list. A simple probing question like, "Why would you say that?" or "Tell me more about that," or "What changed to make you feel that way?" can keep them rolling.

Sometimes it's as simple as "Wow!" "Really?" "Huh." "No way!" "That's hilarious!" You're just giving them a verbal nudge to keep going. If you've never tried this, I dare you to try it. Practice with your spouse or with a friend. You could keep them talking for hours with just those five phrases. And, after, they'll thank you for the great conversation!

Questions are powerful. In his excellent book, *How to Become a Rainmaker*, Jeffery Fox said, "Customers love questions. Customers love to talk. Customers feel more secure with the salesperson who asks questions and listens and takes notes. Asking too few questions is asking to fail."

After you ask good questions, it's time to ***listen***.

CHAPTER 21

LISTENING

Right behind questioning on the list of things salespeople think they are better at than they are, is **listening**. And it's not just salespeople. In a recent survey by Accenture, 96% of global professionals consider themselves good listeners. I think you'd agree that there is no way that many people are good listeners. I hope that in the last chapter, I convinced you that if you ask good questions, your customers will tell you everything you need to know to develop solid and profitable partnerships with them. But, if you don't develop the skill of **listening to what they say**, everything I am recommending to help you become better at selling is worthless.

I don't think the problem in sales conversations is that the salesperson doesn't care or is distracted, which happens in other types of conversations. I think the two most significant barriers to effective listening when you are selling are:

1) Your mind is racing ahead to the solutions, products, and services you want to pitch, and

2) While the other person is answering your last question, you're thinking about the next question instead of listening to what they are saying.

So, here are some recommendations for becoming a better listener in your sales conversations:

Be patient. You'll get your chance to talk about your products and services. But, if you jump into that too early, you will most likely miss some crucial information your customer will share with you if you hold your horses. In medical terms, don't **prescribe** before you **diagnose**.

I love this quote from B2B sales coach Anthony Iannarino: "We love what we sell. We are fire-breathing, proselytizing true believers. Wonderful. But save your recommendation as to the right solution for your dream client until it makes sense; it doesn't make sense to present until you have diagnosed your client's issues, problems, and challenges."

Take notes. Taking notes will not just help you remember the details of the conversation later; it also helps you better understand what is being said. Taking notes engages a different part of the brain than auditory listening. Taking notes forces you to decipher what is important about what the customer is saying and begin organizing it in ways that make sense to you. It's also a tremendously respectful thing to do. Often, when I take out my notepad and ask if it's ok to take notes, I see my customer sit up a little in their chair. You can see it in their face

– they like that someone cares enough about what they think to write it down. No one at home is taking notes when they speak!

I like to take notes in one color pen during the sales conversation, and then later, when I get back to my car, to add notes in a different color pen about my impressions of what was said and any commitments I made to follow up. It's easy for me to forget if I don't make a record of it.

Practice "Active Listening." Active listening means that instead of only gathering details, you consciously try to understand the customer's message thoroughly. Pay attention to their body language, use of sarcasm, and changes in energy levels. Acknowledge that you are listening by nodding and dropping the occasional "Uh-huh."

Since the goal is understanding them, it helps to summarize occasionally and confirm that what you are hearing is what they intend to communicate. Saying something like, "So, what I'm hearing is …" Sometimes they say, "Exactly!" and sometimes they say, "No, no, no, that's not what I mean …" Either one of those answers helps you significantly.

Listen for Gaps. The above advice is about *how* to listen. Let's talk about *what you should be listening for.* As you ask questions about your customer, their business, their goals, etc., you will learn how things are now and how they want things to be. Listen for the gaps between the current state and the desired state. Those gaps are the opportunity for you to add value. Hopefully, your products, services, or advice will help customers bridge the gap between how things are now and how they wish things were.

After you have asked great open-ended questions and listened carefully to what the customer has to say, it's time to share your ideas on how your products or services can help them reach their goals.

The best way I know how to do that is to tell them some *stories*!

CHAPTER 22

TELLING STORIES

Storytelling is as crucial in selling as it is in effective public speaking. Except, when speaking to an audience, you usually tell stories about yourself and your experiences, and in a sales conversation, you should tell stories about other customers and their experiences.

The most powerful stories you could tell a prospective customer are stories about another customer, *just like them*, who benefited from using one of your products, services, or ideas.

When starting in sales, you won't have an extensive catalog of stories from your customer base, so you must rely on stories you've gathered from co-workers, crossline friends, supervisors, trainers, etc. But, as quickly as possible, you need to start building a portfolio of stories and examples of other customers you know whom you've helped, whose lives and businesses have been transformed by purchasing the products or services you sell.

Over time, that *portfolio of stories* will be more valuable to your sales efforts than the *portfolio of products* you sell.

Sentences like this are powerful: "I have a customer who was in the same situation as you, and when they started using this product, they got extraordinary results."

Stories are so psychologically and emotionally powerful. They let the customer know that they are not alone. And stories can dissolve doubt in the new customer's mind that using this product or making a change might not work. Stories are far more effective in selling than statistics and studies. They make the decision to buy seem like a personal thing, which, of course, it is. And stories often help customers connect the dots to the cost of not taking action.

A few years ago, I was proposing my training to the Child Nutrition department at a large school district with 34 schools. By asking good questions, I discovered the director wanted to improve communication in the department, reduce turnover, serve breakfast and lunch to more children, and improve the image of the nutrition program in the minds of the parents and community. I told her stories about how I had helped other school districts accomplish those things by training the kitchen managers at their school sites to become better leaders. When managers develop better leadership skills, everything improves in areas like teamwork, quality, and customer service. The director hired me to create and present a series of training classes called "Leadership Skills for School Nutrition Professionals." (Keep in mind that she didn't *have* to do this training. It wasn't required or mandated by the district or the USDA, but she was convinced I could help her bridge the gap between her current situation and her desired situation).

So, I facilitated four 2-hour training workshops over four months for her managers. We covered great topics like the difference between management and leadership, driving change, setting high standards, creating a customer service culture, holding people accountable, developing trust, teamwork, and bringing out the best in people. A year later, she measured the results. Some of the benefits of training like that can be hard to measure, but there were some tangible results. They had a massive drop-off in turnover and a significant decrease in the number of complaining calls from parents to their central office. And most importantly, they had more than a 20% increase in the number of meals served. That equates to tens of thousands more meals being served to the hungry children of that community, and the only thing they changed was providing their managers with some impactful leadership training.

A lot of good things come out of a situation like that. The director has a sense of satisfaction from having the courage to take action that moves the needle. As you might imagine, she is now a HUGE raving fan of my training. I likewise get enormous personal satisfaction knowing that what I do makes a difference.

But the most significant benefit to me was the ***value of the success story***. I have told that story to other school districts, ***just like them***, who were looking for improvement. I have since been able to sell my leadership training services to dozens of other school districts nationwide. It's good for those departments, the families they serve, and my business.

Leverage your success stories. Do it with humility but with confidence. I call it tooting your own horn without blowing it!

Stories are powerful, especially when they include quantifiable results. It also works well to predict customer results with strategies like *dollarizing*.

CHAPTER 23

DOLLARIZING

A compelling way to demonstrate the value you bring to a customer is a strategy called ***dollarizing***. Dollarizing communicates the economic benefit of purchasing and utilizing a product or service to a customer. If you sell to a B2B customer, this is often literally, "Here's how much money you could make with this business strategy." If you sell directly to a consumer, it may be *savings* in dollars, time, or some other quantifiable measure.

When you ask a customer to make a purchasing decision based on non-economic factors like features and benefits instead of economic factors like profit, they have no choice but to keep looking at the price. The price of something, especially to a business, should only be relevant as it relates to economic value. If you can put a dollar amount on the benefit of purchasing and implementing your products or services, you should.

For example, when I worked in food industry sales, my employer launched an initiative to sell more products. The marketing department created a piece of countertop equipment made for warming and serving soup. It had two 2-gallon pots, ladles, and a sneeze guard and was covered with appealing graphics. It looked nice.

The problem was that they wanted the sales team to go out and sell it to foodservice operators for $2,000 each! TWO GRAND! That's a LOT of money to pay for an electric soup pot!

So, the entire nationwide sales team was instructed to get out there and sell this equipment. Well, no one sold any because none of our customers wanted it. Then the senior management team said we *HAD* to sell them or wouldn't get our annual bonuses. Each salesperson had to sell eight during the fiscal year to unlock their bonus, which could be tens of thousands of dollars. That got my attention. So, I started selling them, but not like the marketing department wanted us to, talking about the soup's taste and the brand's power. I **dollarized**.

I would show the equipment to the owners of restaurants, truck stops, and regional restaurant chains, and the dining managers at hospital, college, military, and factory cafeterias, and break down the **economics**:

"Imagine selling just 2 gallons of soup from each pot daily. With $2.00 profit for every 8-oz. cup of soup, that's $128 of profit a day. You'd make back your $2,000 investment in 16 days and put an extra $46,000 in your pocket in the next year!

"That's enough to buy a new car every year!" I'd tell them. "That's enough to send your kid to college! That's not a soup pot! That's an ATM!"

I didn't sell a unit every time with that approach, but I sold a lot. More than any of my coworkers. This next part was a little embarrassing, but at the National Sales Meeting, the company president got me up in front of everyone and put a medallion around my neck like Han Solo at the end of Star Wars. Better than the medallion was the big bonus I unlocked!

The next fiscal year, they ran a sales contest. The first salesperson in the country who sold eight soup merchandisers won a free cruise for themselves and a guest. They announced it by email at 7:00 am one day, and I sold eight units before noon. Ask me sometime to see the pictures from our beautiful free cruise to Cozumel, Mexico! (Wait - not free. Nothing's free. "At no cost to us!")

I hope you're catching the point of the story. It's about being smart about **what you sell** and **how you sell it**.

My struggling co-workers would ask me, "How in the world do you sell so much equipment?" I would explain, "I don't sell equipment. None of my customers want equipment. I sell **profit**."

Before you think I'm a genius for that strategy, you should know I didn't make that up. I didn't make up any of these techniques and approaches. Like you are right now, I picked up books and tried to learn from others with more experience. In one of the books I read, I ran across a story about Tom Watson, Jr., the son of the founder of IBM and the CEO of the company in the 1950s and 1960s.

In the days before personal computing, when only big companies bought computers, he was asked how it felt to be the world's biggest seller of computers. He replied, "We don't sell computers. We **make** computers. But we **sell** customer growth by applying them." Brilliant. That's where I got the idea. If it works for computers, it can work for soup pots. And it can work for your business too!

Your customers probably don't want protein shakes. They want to be healthier without having to drink something that tastes bad. They don't want laundry detergent; they want clean clothes that smell good. They don't want shampoo; they want their hair to look great. They don't want lawn care; they want their property to look great without doing it themselves. They don't want insurance; they want peace of mind for their family's future. They don't want dinner at a restaurant; they want a friendly dining experience that makes them feel special. Sell *what they want*, not the product or service, and put a dollar or time value on it, and you will smoke your competitors.

Once you've asked good questions, listened, and positioned your products or services as part of a winning strategy, the last thing you may need to do before launching a partnership is to **address some of the customer's concerns**.

CHAPTER 24

ADDRESSING CONCERNS

Most books or training programs on selling have an extensive section on "Handling Objections." The basic idea is arming salespeople with slick tricks to convince buyers to buy something they don't want. I've heard them all: The boomerang method, deflection, reframing, the conditional close, and the L.A.I.R. Method, where you **L**isten, **A**cknowledge, **I**dentify objection, and **R**everse it! Sounds more like a wrestling move than an honest conversation.

Once I developed a win/win consultative mindset, learned to ask good questions, and aligned my selling efforts with customers' wants, I didn't need any of that nonsense.

I love this perspective from Charles H. Green, the CEO of Trusted Advisor Associates:

"At the outset of a professional relationship, we bring some strong ideas about how to add value. So do our clients. This is as it should be. Working collaboratively with the client to take the best of both perspectives creates maximum value. The concept of 'objections' undermines that potential synergy. It suggests that selling is a struggle of ideas, a contest of wills, and that our job is to persuade the client of the superiority of ours. Hence we get objection-'handling.' Like snake-'handling,' it has overtones of danger - if we don't know the tricks of savvy handlers, we're likely to get bitten. But we don't need to go there. If we can approach the client with an open-minded, curiosity-driven, adventuresome, mutual attitude of discovery, then 'objections' no longer look like snakes. They are simply emotional statements about the buyer's readiness. They are information, not attacks. Of course, there will always be timing, budget, politics, and alignment issues. We need to identify them along with the client proactively. To do any less is unprofessional."

That is so good, and I couldn't agree more. To me, this step in the process is just a continued conversation. Talk about it. If the product or service is a bad fit, I don't want to sell it because that would hurt my relationship with the customer and my reputation in the marketplace. If there are questions, doubts, or concerns about fit, let's chat about it. Sometimes the customer has a misconception about something. In that case, I do my best to clarify. If they are skeptical, I may tell a few more stories and examples of other people, *just like them*, who moved forward with me and were glad they did. If it's a timing issue – let's wait. I'm not in a hurry. If they are afraid to change, it's my job to help them understand how risky that can be.

American computer scientist and U.S. Navy Rear Admiral Grace Hopper famously said, "The most dangerous phrase in the language is 'we've always done it this way.'"

Part of my role as a strategic resource is to help my customers think through the risk and cost of changing AND the risk and expense of *not changing*. Most understand that organizations that embrace change and try new things thrive, and organizations that cling to the old way of doing things usually die.

I commit to be alongside them every step of the way and promise to do whatever it takes to make things right if there is a problem. That is usually enough to get the right customers to move forward with the right products. This whole communication process builds trust, and that's what is needed to handle concerns effectively!

Good luck with your selling efforts! I hope this section of the book helps you. Now that we've covered Public Speaking and Selling, the next section of this book covers *six other types of essential conversations in which communication skills play a huge role*.

ESSENTIAL CONVERSATIONS

Now that we've done a deep dive into public speaking and selling, in Part III of this book, we'll get into other types of essential conversations you are likely to have in your life repeatedly. In these conversations, your ability to organize your thoughts and communicate verbally with power, authenticity, and effectiveness will play an enormous role in your success, happiness, and peace of mind.

The critical conversations we'll dig into are communicating with strangers, in interviews, with difficult people, in your relationships, as parents, and finally, to the most important person.

CHAPTER 25

COMMUNICATING WITH STRANGERS

While you are sure to have plenty of public speaking and selling opportunities, the most frequent public communication you can and should participate in is *communication with strangers*.

Most people prefer to avoid this type of communication almost as much as public speaking. They walk around daily, pretending they don't see the people around them. They'll sit on a plane, less than an inch away from another human being, and not say a word. They'll stand in line for hours waiting to ride roller coasters, passing the same people repeatedly in the queue, and never even acknowledge or engage with them. It's weird, unnatural, and dehumanizing. And it's incredibly unhealthy.

We live in a bizarre time in history where individuals are "connected" to more people than ever yet feel more isolated and lonelier than ever. According to an advisory released in May 2023 by U.S. Surgeon General Dr. Vivek Murthy, there is an *epidemic of loneliness* in the United States, and lacking connection can increase the risk of premature death to levels comparable to smoking 15 cigarettes a day. The report, entitled *Our Epidemic of Loneliness and Isolation*, warns that the physical consequences of poor connections with others can be devastating, including a 29% increased risk of heart disease, a 32% increased risk of stroke, and a 50% increased risk of developing dementia for older adults.

Meeting new people is the quickest and most logical way to eliminate loneliness, but few people do it. Your reluctance to talk to strangers could literally be killing you.

Avoiding connecting with and talking to strangers isn't just unhealthy; it's unwise. I assume that because you're reading this book, you have some things you want to accomplish – dreams and goals that require you to learn to communicate more effectively. It is doubtful that you will reach those goals with your existing circle of influence. You will need to work with others to accomplish anything significant in your life, and chances are you don't yet know all the people you need to know. You must network, meet new people, and talk to them.

This is especially true if you want to build something – a business, a church, a charity, or a team. No one has ever accomplished anything extraordinary by themselves, and the bigger your dreams and goals, the more people you will need to meet and get to know.

Talking to strangers is unusual psychologically because people commonly report that they don't like doing it, but they also say they feel energized when they do. Let's look at why people don't want to talk to strangers, some benefits of communicating with people you don't yet know, and some tips to help you have productive, enjoyable conversations.

WHY PEOPLE DON'T TALK TO STRANGERS

They Don't Want to Be Weird. Nobody likes it when people think you're a weirdo, but talking to strangers isn't as weird as ignoring them. The emotion behind that fear is the same as in Chapter 2 – you care too much about what others think of you. The truth is that people simply aren't thinking about you as much as you expect. At this very moment, no one in the world is likely thinking about you. Not a single person. Others are far too focused on thinking about themselves.

One way to overcome this fear is to build your dream and think about what you really want out of life; your life's purpose. Maybe it's influence in the lives of others, financial prosperity that allows you to make a difference, building a team that changes the world, staying true to your spiritual convictions, or earning the respect of the people you respect. The bigger your dream gets, the less the fear of a stranger's opinion of you will matter.

We've Been Taught That Strangers Are Dangerous. If you grew up in the 80s or later, you were indoctrinated with the idea of "Stranger Danger!" It's a misguided and outdated strategy intended to protect children, but it ignores the reality that more than 90% of harm done to children is perpetrated by people they know. Instead of teaching kids to avoid dangerous situations, it taught them a deep fear of strangers, condemning several generations of people to lives of needless isolation.

Of course, you need to exercise wisdom, and there are parts of the city you live in that you should probably avoid after dark. But the person next to you on your flight or in line behind you at lunch is unlikely to kidnap you. Your lifelong exaggerated desire for security limits your chances of success in life.

One of my favorite quotations is from Helen Keller, who wrote, "Security is mostly a superstition. It does not exist in nature, nor do the children of men as a whole experience it. Avoiding danger is no safer in the long run than outright exposure. Life is either a daring adventure or nothing."

We've Been Conditioned to Focus on Differences. There are strong forces in the world today that want to divide people. People divided by skin color, economic class, cultural background, political party, age, and religious beliefs are easier to control and manipulate. And people who look at issues from an "us versus them" perspective are suspicious and fearful of strangers.

But don't forget that ***you are a spirit***. So is everyone you meet, and they are not that different from you. Maya Angelou famously said, "We are more alike, my friends, than we are unalike."

We Don't Expect Strangers to Like Us. Researchers have discovered a "liking gap," a disparity between how much you think people like you when they meet you versus the reality. In many studies, people consistently underestimate how much others like them after an initial conversation. You're pretty awesome. Let your light shine.

Most People Never Learned How to Talk to Strangers. Unfortunately, talking to strangers is on the long list of crucial skills not taught in schools. I'm sure you learned how to play the recorder or that mitochondria are the powerhouse of the cell but not the power of communicating with strangers. I'll give you some tips to help you get better at this vital skill, but first, let's look at some of the benefits of learning to communicate more effectively with strangers.

BENEFITS OF LEARNING TO COMMUNICATE WITH STRANGERS

You Will Develop a Critical Success Skill. The ability to carry on a conversation with another person is one of the most crucial skills a person can possess. This will almost certainly have more to do with your success and happiness than skills like interior decorating, fishing, or hitting a golf ball. Communicating with strangers is something you should practice every day.

You Could Meet a Person You Need in Your Life. Some of my closest friends were once strangers I dared to converse with. My wife was once a college freshman I didn't know to whom I introduced myself. There isn't a single person on my business team who I knew when I started the business. Talking to strangers changed the trajectory of my life. I would have nothing I have and be nothing I am today without my willingness to talk to strangers.

You'll Learn Things You Didn't Know. I have learned so many things about many topics by talking to strangers. Far more than I ever learned in school.

It Will Improve Your Mood. Studies have shown that talking to strangers increases your sense of belonging and makes you happier and more optimistic. You'll feel good about yourself that you didn't just stay wrapped up in your private world.

You Can Connect People to One Another. One of the things I love to do is connect a person I just met with another of my friends. I love this quote from Tim Sanders' book *Love is the Killer App*:

"While we collect marbles, baseball cards, and antiques in order to hold on to them while they increase in value, the purpose of collecting contacts is to give them away – to match them with other contacts. Whenever you introduce people, instead of one plus one equaling two, it equals two to infinity – because when we make a successful connection, we are helping create that one-in-a-million business relationship with which we are forever associated and that may connect us to myriad new network nodes."

You'll Uncover Opportunity. I have stumbled across very profitable business opportunities while talking to a stranger. Some of my best customers and clients were strangers with whom I initiated a conversation.

It Puts Your Problems into Perspective. I've learned from talking to thousands of strangers that people carry heavy burdens. I've met extraordinary people who are going through unbelievably difficult circumstances. Those interactions make me grateful for my many blessings and relatively insignificant challenges.

You Might Be the Person Someone Else Desperately Needs to Meet. I have met many strangers who needed someone like me in their life. I'm thankful for the opportunity to start what might be a lifelong friendship or offer encouragement to someone who needs it.

Your Friend Group Will Grow and Spread. Most people have made friends in their life based on proximity. Your close friends are probably people you were near at school, church, or work. There is nothing wrong with that, but there exists an enormous possible friend group for you that is based on your future more than your past. By talking to strangers, I have become close friends with people who aren't necessarily from my town but who are *on the same path*, headed toward a common destination. I've made friends around the country and the world. One of my goals is to have friends in every major city to have cool people to hang out with anywhere I go!

A very different kind of friendship is possible with someone who shares your values, priorities, standards, and direction than with someone who happens to have been planted in the same garden as you have. By talking to LOTS of strangers, I have found many of those rare gem individuals whom I really click with and am aligned with spiritually, and it's gratifying.

You'll Meet Some Fascinating People. I've had interesting conversations with people who work for the government, magicians, politicians, foreign government workers, ministers, cops, students, business owners, and many military personnel. One recent guy I met told me he was a writer for WWE professional wrestling. Jokingly, I said, "Are you saying wrestling is fake?" He got a severe look on his face and said, "It's *not* fake. It's scripted. Those are world-class athletes putting their bodies on the line to entertain their fans." I stood corrected, and we had a fascinating conversation about determining the winners, losers, and champions in pro wrestling.

I love this perspective from *The Power of Strangers: The Benefits of Connecting in a Suspicious World* by Joe Keohane:

> "When you talk to people you don't know, you learn
> that everyone has a bit of gold; everyone has at least one

thing to say that will surprise you, amuse you, horrify you, edify you. They tell you things, usually with minimal prodding, and sometimes those things can deepen you, and awaken you to the richness and the grace and even the pain of the human experience."

You'll Help Move Our Society in the Right Direction. When you talk to strangers, you'll see that we are all more alike than you ever imagined. You'll meet parents who want what's best for their kids, workers who want more control over their lives, and people who love their country and communities. Everyone is unique and special, but they all want happiness, to do meaningful work, healthy relationships, fulfillment, peace of mind, and to leave a legacy.

One of the best tweets I've read came from comic actor Rob Schneider, whom I think nailed it with this: "If you turn off the news and talk to your neighbors, you'll find that our country is far more harmonious than you're being told."

By getting out of your isolated private world and genuinely connecting with your fellow humans, you are helping to eliminate stereotypes and racism, adding your unique flavor to society, and being a light in a dark world. It matters. You matter.

So, hopefully, we are on the same page that you should develop the skill of communicating with strangers. But, if you don't yet have this habit, it will be a little awkward and difficult at first, like all good habits are. Here are some ideas that should help:

TIPS FOR COMMUNICATING WITH STRANGERS EFFECTIVELY

Work on Breaking the Ice. Until everyone around you has read this book, you'll have to be the one who gets conversations started. If you're new to developing the habit of talking to strangers, you'll likely run into someone you'd like to have a conversation with, but you don't know how to get it started. That's natural. Try different things to see what works for you. Some things that work for me:

+ Make a humorous comment about something going on around you. If I'm on a flight or in a store and something unusual happens, it's the perfect chance to chat with whoever is nearby.

+ Ask a question. Intellectual curiosity is essential to develop, as it keeps your mind sharp and in active mode instead of passive mode. So, ask questions. I often ask if they like their brand of laptop computer or their car or if there is a restaurant in the area they recommend, and it gets a conversation rolling.

+ Pay a compliment. Complimenting someone makes both parties feel good and is a great way to start a conversation. I often compliment someone and then follow it up with a question. "I love your truck. Do you need it for your work, or do you like driving a big vehicle?" or "I like how you handled that situation. Do you work in a leadership role?" Just be sincere with your compliments.

Have an "Elevator Speech" Ready to Go. You've probably heard of the idea of an elevator speech or pitch. If you were on an elevator ride with someone for thirty seconds, could you clearly and concisely share who you are or what you do? If someone asks you what you do, and you give them a rambling answer about what you do full-time and in your spare time, what you used to do, and why you left your last employer – you've lost their interest. Think through a concise way you'd like to introduce yourself to others. Keep it brief and positive. Like Albert Einstein said, "If you can't explain it simply, you don't understand it well enough."

You may want to practice this. Video record yourself sharing how you would introduce yourself to a stranger and watch it. Send the video to someone you trust and respect and ask for feedback. They may notice things you don't. Remember, 7% of your influence comes from your words, 38% comes from your tone of voice, and 55% is what your body does while you are saying it.

Put a Smile on Your Face. Smiling indicates warmth and friendliness, but it also affects your brain and the brains of others. Marco Iacoboni, a neuroscientist at UCLA, studied brain activity and discovered that smiling is contagious. In his book, *Mirroring People: The Science of How We Connect to Others*, he wrote, "When I see you smiling, my mirror neurons for smiling fire up, too, initiating a cascade of neural activity that evokes the feeling we typically associate with a smile. I don't need to infer what you're feeling; I experience immediately and effortlessly what you are experiencing."

Some people struggle to smile. I have friends who are good, loving people, but their personality is sterner than others. Smiling doesn't come naturally to them. My advice to those people? ***Change***. Work on smiling. It's a skill that can be developed, just like eye contact. The good news is that smiling will make you more attractive to others, make an excellent first impression, and make you feel better. Thich Nhat Hanh said, "Sometimes your joy is the source of your smile, but sometimes your smile can be the source of your joy."

Find Common Ground. One of the best ways to connect with someone is to find something you have in common with them. It's fun to figure out what I have in common with someone, and sometimes it's easy. I always talk to anyone I see wearing some merch from one of my beloved sports teams – the Detroit Lions, Tigers, Pistons, Redwings, or the Michigan Wolverines! I have much in common with those fans, mainly decades of heartbreaking disappointment. I find that I have things in common with most people, like being married, having kids, living in the same part of the country, or having similar career experiences. If nothing else, we are literally standing on common ground because we are at the same place at the same time, so talking about where we each are coming from and going is easy.

Listen More Than You Talk. You may have heard the expression that God gave you two ears and one mouth for a reason – and you should use them in that ratio.

Be Yourself. This is a recurring theme in this book, but please don't try to be someone or something you're not. You are unique and amazing; no one who has ever lived has your particular combination of traits, personality, passions, and ideas. Let your authentic self shine, and you will attract the right kind of people who want to know someone like you.

Take a Sincere Interest in Other People. I see a lot of articles and social media posts about "How to Be the Most Interesting Person in the Room." That's a shallow goal, as it doesn't accomplish anything other than feeding your ego. I would much rather be perceived as being inter*ested* than interest*ing*. Show some empathy and try to understand where others are coming from.

Don't Complain. When I talk to a stranger, they often complain about some situation or person. It's easy and tempting to jump in and add your complaints. Unfortunately, complainers turn people off, even if they are complainers themselves. Instead, try to turn the conversation in a positive direction by being a ***good finder*** – someone who finds the good in every person and every situation. It's a rare trait and one that is very attractive.

Don't Be Creepy. Talking to strangers isn't weird, but you can ***make it*** weird. Don't ask overly personal questions or share excessively personal details about your life. Practice good hygiene and dress nicely. Avoid talking about topics other people find disturbing. Respect people's personal space. If you wonder if you are giving off a creepy vibe, ask someone who knows you well to be honest with you.

Be Courteous. Our society has become less courteous, which makes it stand out more when someone is polite. So, avoid behaviors like correcting people, interrupting, looking at your phone while talking to someone else, or one-upping their stories with bigger and better stories of your own.

Don't Worry About It When You Meet a Jerk. An overwhelming majority of the people I have conversed with were polite, engaging, and interesting. Humans are social animals and crave interaction. Occasionally, I've met a total jerk. When I ask them a question, they say, "Why? Are you writing a book?" (Ironically – yes. I'm writing a book). Or they turn away from me or walk away. One dude on a flight pulled his scarf up and wrapped it around his face so he wouldn't have to talk to me. It doesn't bother me in the least. It says nothing about me and everything about them. Those are people I don't want to be friends with anyway, and I honestly feel sorry for them.

Exchange Contact Information. If you have a good conversation with someone, asking them if they'd like to exchange information is perfectly socially acceptable. I've missed doing this before and regretted it. When I just walked away from a fantastic conversation with an extraordinary person, I almost always think later of how I could add value to their life if I only had a way to reach them. So, now I say, "I've really enjoyed talking with you. I'd love to stay in touch. Can I send you my contact information?" I text them with my cell number or email them, depending on which is more appropriate, and now a conversation has turned into a valued connection!

Talking to strangers can and will change your life. I sincerely hope you add this to the communication skills you are developing. The next chapter will focus on a specific type of conversation that requires specific strategies and skills – ***interviewing***.

CHAPTER 26

COMMUNICATING IN INTERVIEWS

All of us will participate in interviews in our lives, either as the interviewer or the interviewee, or both. But people rarely do it often enough to become proficient, so focusing on the mindset and strategies of communicating effectively in an interview setting is essential.

I've only participated in a handful of job interviews as a candidate, but I have conducted hundreds of interviews with prospective candidates who were seeking employment with an organization for which I worked or who were looking to start a business of their own working with my team. I've also mentored many people going through the job search or interview process in their careers, and I've seen some patterns in what strategies work best.

THE JOB SEARCH

As I've mentioned, I am a big proponent of self-employment. If you are willing to work hard and learn to be an effective communicator, I think working for yourself offers you the most opportunity. However, depending on your dreams, goals, priorities, and industry, that's not a good option for many people. There are not a lot of self-employed teachers, pharmacists, firefighters, dental hygienists, or hundreds of other professions. And even if your dream is to be self-employed, it's often wise to work a job for a while as you launch your business in addition to your full-time employment.

The process of finding a job has changed a lot in my lifetime. In the mid-90s, when I was a college instructor, I taught a class on interviewing skills – *COM234 – Fundamentals of Interviewing*. (I suspect you had no idea there were college classes on this subject). Back then, I ran across a statistic that 80% of new hires were for unadvertised positions. That was a shockingly high number. So, I used to recommend that people network with people they know and meet instead of sending hundreds of resumes to companies because 99% of job seekers were going after 20% of the jobs listed or advertised somewhere, and those jobs were probably not the best opportunities out there. Well, the internet has changed everything, and now between social media platforms like LinkedIn and thousands of industry-specific job boards, most job opportunities are listed somewhere. I still maintain, however, that the *best* opportunities working for the *best* organizations get filled quickly. HR managers and executives who are hiring know about the opening long before it's posted and start asking around in their network for a qualified candidate who is a known quantity. Many of the jobs listed are the positions organizations have trouble filling and keeping people in.

Some organizations create a position when they find a good potential employee they think could add value to their team. Every job I've had came either from someone I knew who recommended me to their boss, or someone I knew recruiting me to leave my job and work for them, sometimes creating a new position specifically for me.

Some of the things I learned about job searches include:

Don't Rely Exclusively on Your Resume. Your resume can be a helpful tool once you find a position to apply for, but it won't do much to help you find an opportunity to pursue. And some of you – let's be honest – have a resume that's not all that impressive. I'm sure you've done some great things, but do you want a piece of paper to do your talking for you? If it's in a stack with 60 other resumes, what are the chances yours will be the most impressive?

As much as possible, I recommend taking the bull by the horns and making your job search personal and aggressive. There are two primary ways you can do that:

1) Talk to every person you know who might have contacts in your profession and ask them if they know anyone who might be hiring.

2) Be proactive and meet some strangers and ask them.

I know that strategy sounds wild, but it *always* works for those with the guts to do it. I have a friend who was looking to make a career change and asked me for advice. He has a magnetic personality, a smile that lights up a room, a strong work ethic, is a great leader and coach, and has phenomenal people skills. His resume, though, was not so hot. He has a college degree from the 80s in an obscure and irrelevant major and has worked a series of not-very-impressive positions at not-very-impressive employers. He told me that he had emailed his resume to hundreds of companies looking for a sales position (or any position) and hadn't even scrounged up an interview.

I asked him, "Why on earth are you letting your resume do the talking for you instead of *you* doing the talking for you?" I told him that I knew a strategy guaranteed to land a job quickly, but it takes *courage* and *verbal communication*, and I would only tell him about it if he promised to try it, which he did. This is what I recommended:

Tomorrow, I want you to wear a suit and tie and go to the restaurant in your community where successful people go to lunch. (Every town has at least one). Walk in at 12:15 and look around. Pick out the nicest-dressed, most professional-looking person in the restaurant and walk up to them and say, "Excuse me, I don't want to interrupt your lunch, but you look like a successful business professional." Introduce yourself and say, "I am seeking a new career opportunity. Do you know of any growing organizations that might be interested in hiring a bold, confident, articulate person who isn't afraid to talk to strangers?"

He thought I was nuts, but I guaranteed him that if he was willing to do that until it worked, there was no way he would ever make it to 20 conversations before he landed a new job.

I *double-dog-dared* him to try it, so then he had no choice.

Give the guy credit – he did it. He walked in, approached a well-dressed man sitting at a table with another man, and said what I recommended. The guy started laughing and said, "Wow. Pretty impressive. Here's my card. Call me tomorrow, and we'll talk."

After a great phone conversation and an interview, he was offered a job and started working for the man's company by the end of the week!

I know that's not how people usually find a job. *That's the point*.

One of the success lessons I have learned is to **observe the masses and do the opposite**. It is rarely wise to do things like everyone else does, especially if you want to stand out! If you are in the market for a new job, I dare you to try it too! (Some of you are too afraid of what people think to try this approach. You need to go back and read Chapter 2).

Make Your Resume Stand Out. While I don't think most of you should let your resume do the talking for you, you can still use strategies to make your resume stand out from the rest of the pile on a hiring manager's desk. There is no shortage of articles and blogs on this subject, but I've found one strategy I've never seen recommended anywhere else that works great. It's a way of better utilizing the "work history" section of your resume. Most people list the employer, years they worked there, title, and responsibilities – **what they did**. I recommend listing all of that but adding one sentence. Right after *what you did*, add **<u>what you learned</u>** in that position. So, for example, one of the items on my resume is:

United States Slo-Pitch Softball Association
Umpire
Summers 1987-1992
Put myself through college as a softball umpire. Officiated over 700 softball games every summer for five years. *Learned how to make quick decisions in high-pressure situations.*

What I did wasn't that impressive, but *what I learned* was! Every job interview I've had since, every interviewer has read that and said, "Huh. I never thought about that. That must be a hard job. I bet you learned a lot from that experience."

Every job in my resume's work history section lists *what I learned in that position*. Here are some other examples:

Corporate Trainer – (After listing job responsibilities and accomplishments) – *Developed the ability to integrate training programs into corporate culture and structure, successfully navigate corporate politics, and equip salespeople to succeed personally and professionally.*

Sales Professional – *Developed high proficiency in Consultative Selling, leading to rapid sales growth, often doubling my sales numbers yearly. Developed expertise in cross-functional, cross-divisional teamwork within a Fortune 500 corporation.*

University Instructor – *Learned how to engage learners practically, making them want to learn and grow.*

This strategy accomplishes two things:

1) It demonstrates that you are a lifelong learner who is constantly growing and developing new skills and capabilities, and

2) It argues that each of your previous positions was training and preparing you for this current opportunity!

BEING INTERVIEWED

Going on a job interview can be a stressful experience, depending on how desperate you are for the job. Here are a few things I'd recommend to ensure you get the best results:

Be Yourself. Most people go into a job interview with one goal – Get. The. Job. That is the wrong goal, in my opinion. You should go into a job interview to find out if the position you are considering is a good fit for you and vice versa. When people are laser-focused on getting the job, they work hard to try to impress the interviewer, which almost always results in them pretending to be something they're not to some degree.

Do you know what's worse than not getting the job? *Getting the wrong job*! When a square peg talks their way into a job requiring them to squeeze into a round hole daily, it's a recipe for unhappiness and disengagement. This is why so many people hate their jobs because they went into the job interview with the wrong goal!

Gallup recently released their 2022 "State of the Global Workplace" report. They found that, along with dissatisfaction, workers are experiencing staggering rates of both disengagement and unhappiness. 60% of people reported being emotionally detached at work, and 19% reported being completely miserable. Only 33% reported feeling engaged at work. In the U.S. specifically, 50% of workers reported feeling stressed at their jobs daily, 41% as being worried, 22% as sad, and 18% as angry.

What is remarkable to me is that *each* of those people **chose** to work at their employer! They all interviewed for those jobs, tried to make a good impression, got the ***wrong position*** for them, and ended up

158

trapped in a bad situation. The best way to avoid this is to be yourself and consider *fit*. Consider whether this position would fit your values, goals, skills, priorities, and passion, whether you would be a good fit for that organization, and what they want to accomplish. This takes patience, wisdom, and confidence. The beautiful side effect is that your nervousness will vanish because there's nothing to be nervous about.

Ask Good Questions. It would be best if you didn't ask selfish questions about how much vacation they offer or how soon you'll be promoted. Ask questions about *culture*. If you have a passion for personal growth and development (and I assume you do if you're reading this book), ask questions about the degree to which the organization supports learning and development. If you love contributing to your employer's success, ask questions about how someone in the proposed position can move the needle for the organization. Good questions will help you dial in if this is a good fit.

TALENT ACQUISITION

Let's talk about when *you* are doing the recruiting or hiring. You must attract, interview, onboard, and train talented people to accomplish extraordinary things with your organization. Your ability to communicate intelligently and effectively when interviewing others will significantly contribute to your success as an executive or business owner. Here are some things to think about as you find and interview talented people:

Work Your Contact List. You know many people. Former coworkers, sports teammates, your kids' friends' parents, and people with whom you went to high school or college. Interviewing someone you already know for a position with your team cuts through a lot of the interpersonal mystery because you have a preexisting connection and already know something about their personality and character.

And remember, everyone you know knows people you don't know. Ask for referrals from the people you respect. If you get some recommendations, use the name of the person who referred them when you contact them.

Be On the Lookout for Talent Everywhere You Go. You never know when you will meet an extraordinary person who might be perfect for your team. One of my clients, a School Nutrition Director at a large school district, told me she had the most challenging time finding good people to work in her district's cafeterias and asked for my advice.

I asked her, "What's your strategy for talent acquisition?"

"Huh?" she said.

"Hiring." I clarified. "What's your strategy for hiring people?"

"Well, we put 'Now Hiring' on our website," she replied.

"Well," I said, "You're going to have to be more proactive than that!"

I asked her, "When you go to restaurants, do you ever get excellent service? "Sure," she said.

I told her, "You need to recruit those people!"

I coached her through how I'd do it. I'd compliment the great server and ask if they have kids. If they do, ask them, "How'd you like a job where you never have to work at night again? How about never working a weekend, ever, the rest of your life? What about *every holiday off?* Three weeks off in December for the holidays! Do your kids have Spring Break every year? How'd you like that week off too? Every year! Do you want summers off to be with your family? Ok! Our team members work while their kids or grandkids are at school and are home when the kids are!"

This proposition is compelling for people working nights and weekends while their kids are home. She'd put her best foot forward by featuring the most appealing aspect of the positions she seeks to fill.

One of the benefits of this approach is that when you personally recruit outstanding candidates, you don't even need much of an interview because you are choosing them from the beginning!

I ran into that client a year later at the School Nutrition Association Annual National Conference.

"How's your talent acquisition strategy going?" I asked.

"You wouldn't believe it!" she excitedly replied. "I have recruited more than twenty of the best servers in our county to leave their restaurant jobs and work in our cafeterias!"

"Wow!" I said. "How are they doing?"

"They're some of the best people in our department!" she replied. "They understand customer service, work hard, and are so happy and thankful!"

What a great success story. And what a great leader who's becoming a great communicator.

Be Patient. The biggest mistake I see interviewers make is interviewing three or four people and then hiring the best of that group. They settle for the most adequate, least unappealing of a small sample. Business managers are in a hurry because that open position is putting a strain on the whole department. Business owners are in a hurry because they have such big dreams and goals for growth. But sometimes, you need to slow down to speed up.

Amazon.com founder Jeff Bezos once said, "I'd rather interview 50 people and not hire anyone than hire the wrong person." When I share that in one of my seminars, everyone nods their head at the wisdom of the statement. But how many leaders have ever interviewed 50 people without offering someone a spot on their team? Not very many. But if you've been a leader in the business world for any substantial amount of time, I bet you've experienced the pain and cost of onboarding *the wrong person*. Ouch. Don't offer a position to the first acceptable candidate. That's not what you want. You want ***the right person***.

Know What You're Looking For. It's easy to say, "Find the right person." But what does that mean? It will vary slightly from industry to industry, but I recommend looking for ***attitude***, not ***skills***. The skills required to succeed with your team can probably be taught, and someone with a positive attitude will pick them up quickly. But someone with a negative attitude won't move the needle, no matter how skilled they are. What attitudes should you be looking for?

+ The number one thing I recommend you look for is, *are they happy*? "Come on!" you say, "Happiness?" Yep.

  Happy people make great teammates. They don't bring their drama from home into the workplace. They're comfortable making decisions and don't blame others for their mistakes. They're thankful. Conversely, you can't do anything as a leader to make an unhappy person happy. Unhappy people will drain the life out of your team, no matter how skilled they are.

+ The other most desirable attitude on a business team is *proven initiative*. How have they overcome adversity in their life? Are they resilient? Can they assess a situation and act independently to fix a problem? When have they voluntarily taken on more responsibility to accomplish a team goal? Asking and conversing about those topics will help you discover if you're talking to the right person.

Interviewing is a unique situation that requires specific communication strategies and approaches. Working to communicate better in interviews will profoundly impact your career success.

In the next chapter, we will focus on another situation when good communication skills make a big difference – when *dealing with difficult people*.

CHAPTER 27

COMMUNICATING WITH DIFFICULT PEOPLE

Benjamin Franklin famously said, "In this world, nothing can be said to be certain, except death and taxes." I want to add an item to that list. In this world, you're also certain to deal with **difficult people**.

One of the most popular workshops I do at conferences is called, *I Think I'm Allergic to Nuts! Learning How to Work Productively with People Who Drive You Crazy*. I've been able to help many people reduce stress and improve their quality of life by teaching them to communicate better with the difficult people in their life. And now, dear reader, I'd love to help you do the same!

WHAT ARE DIFFICULT PEOPLE?

I often ask my audiences to think of someone they know who they consider "difficult." Then I ask them to shout out what behaviors or characteristics that person exhibits that make them so difficult. The answers are always the same:

Stubborn, negative, refuses to change, plays mind games, always has to be right, slacker, blames others for their own mistakes, gossips, a moocher, dishonest, manipulative, disagreeable, judgmental, critical, overreactor, close-minded, complainer, grudge-holder, perpetual victim, passive-aggressive, etc.

These people are *everywhere*. And relationships with these people, at work, at church, or God forbid, at home, are exhausting. In their book, *Dealing with People You Can't Stand*, Rick Brinkman and Rich Kirschner said, "Unfortunately, you're going to have to work with jerks, and not just patiently, but productively."

WHY BOTHER?

So why bother dedicating some time and energy to learning how to communicate more effectively with difficult people? In short, if you don't, you're choosing to let these people steal your happiness and peace. Life is too short for that. And you can't just quit your job, church, or business team because there is a difficult person there. Because guess what? There will be difficult people at the next job, church, or business team too!

And the difficult people in your life allow you to develop a valuable skill - learning to communicate with difficult people! You couldn't do it without them.

In his book *Thank You for Being Such a Pain*, Mark Rosen wrote, "Difficult individuals, whether they be relatives, bosses, co-workers, neighbors, or clerks, can be seen as teachers delivering a divine kick in the spiritual butt. The Universe delivers unto us the ideal foe, a person whose characteristics exactly correspond to the places within us that need learning and healing. If we don't learn the lessons they bring, similar problems will perpetually resurface until we do."

WHY DO PEOPLE ACT LIKE THAT?

Why do some people act so problematically? For some, it goes back to how they were raised or unresolved emotional damage they've suffered. As you've probably heard it said, hurting people hurt people, and if you never heal from what hurt you, you'll bleed on people who didn't cut you.

Some difficult people have character flaws that they are letting drive their behavior. In one, or many ways, they never grew up and have immature behavior patterns that are annoying and hurtful to others. Things like jealousy, deceitfulness, cowardice, arrogance, greediness, or spitefulness. These are areas that most people work on and improve in as they move through adolescence and into adulthood. But difficult people stay trapped in those childish emotional mindsets.

Often, negative, angry, selfish behavior comes down to one three-letter word: *Ego*. An ego is a person's self-awareness or self-esteem, and it determines and defines how they interact with others. I have observed that the human ego is of such value to its possessor that they will go to extraordinary lengths to protect it.

Les Giblin, the author of the classic book *The Art of Dealing with People*, says, "We are all ego-hungry. And it is only when this ego is at least partially satisfied that we can forget ourselves, take our attention off ourselves and give it to something else. Only those who have learned to like themselves can be generous and friendly with others." Understanding how a person's ego may be driving their problematic behavior helps you figure out what to do about it.

STRATEGIES TO COMMUNICATE WITH DIFFICULT PEOPLE

Show Some Grace. If a problematic person does something you don't like, and your reaction is to get angry, judge them, gossip about them to others, and hold a grudge – guess what? Who's the difficult person now? Try your best to apply some grace and forgiveness. Give people the same ***room to grow*** that you expect people to give you. You have no idea what that person is going through, what burdens they are carrying, and what pressures they are under. Give grace to others and see if that doesn't dissipate some of your bad feelings.

Some difficult people take perverse pleasure in emotionally torturing others, but most are blissfully unaware of how their behavior is perceived. In her book, *A Survival Guide for Working with Humans*, Gini Graham Scott wrote, "Usually, the difficult person is someone who is working from the negative side of their personality, rather than a conscious desire to be difficult. The person is often unaware of themselves and how they affect others. They also don't realize how harmful their actions are to their own career success." Assume people have good motives until you know otherwise.

Don't Use Labels. Labeling other people based on their problematic behavior doesn't help things. Harvard researcher Amy Gallo, author of *Getting Along: How to Work with Anyone (Even Difficult People)*, makes this excellent point: "Don't use labels. 'Stop being so passive-aggressive!' is a loaded phrase that will only make things worse. I'd be shocked if your colleague said, 'Yeah, you're right. I'll stop.' It's more likely that this request would make them even more angry and defensive, which will stop any sort of positive communication in its tracks."

Chill Out. If you are constantly offended by what other people do and say, you need to *chill out*. The things that get you all worked up and upset say a lot about you. A bizarre *Spirit of Offendedness* is taking over our society. People take offense more and more frequently over things that are less and less significant. Here's the truth you may not like – When you announce to the world, "I'm offended!" what you're saying is, "Hey everybody, since I am such a weak person, and I can't control my emotions, everyone needs to be careful what they say around me and walk on eggshells." Not a very appealing message.

You *choose* the things that you get offended about. That's why it's called "taking offense." You *took it*. So please put it back and lighten up.

It's OK to Distance Yourself. If you were sitting in a room with a smoker, and it bothered you, you'd get up and move. The same is valid with difficult people. As much as possible, I recommend you find ways to spend less time around negative, miserable people. When I learned the degree to which my attitude and happiness were influenced by the

168

people I associated with, I started cutting some people out of my life and pursuing different, healthier relationships.

Don't Enable. It's ok to call people out when they are constantly complaining, venting, or gossiping. I used to work with a woman who would sit in her cubicle, and whenever someone would walk by, she would let out a long, heavy, discouraged sigh. Everything about her said, "Please feel sorry for me." Of course, it was a trap, as she hoped any approaching victim walking by would say, "What's wrong?"

Don't say that to negative people! It's like giving crack to a drug addict!

I took a different approach. I'd say, "Hey, you sound like you need someone to help you cheer up! Let's play a game. It's called Count Your Blessings! You go first!" She stopped making those sighs around me quickly.

People say, "Well, sometimes I just need a shoulder to cry on." I get that's what you *want*, but you *need* someone to help you focus on something more positive. People think "venting" will make them feel better, but it doesn't, and it just pulls you deeper into dark feelings and confirms how bad your life is.

Venting is like ***emotional farting***. It only makes you feel better for a minute, and if you keep doing it around other people, no one will want to be around you.

So, I don't let people "vent" around me for long because it's not good for either of us. You're not doing someone a favor by empowering them to feel bad about their lives and themselves.

Stop Arguing. More than anything in this book, this advice is the hardest for me. I ***love*** arguing. I'm good at arguing. I've taken graduate-level classes in Argumentation and Persuasion. If you and I got into a debate, I'd probably win. I got mad skills. When I was younger, I was so proud of my arguing skills. And then I made a terrible mistake. When I got married, I brought those debating skills into my marriage. *Oh boy.*

When I was a young married guy, I thought if two people disagreed about anything, they should have a debate. I wasn't trying to be a jerk; I thought it was the best way to make decisions. So over and over, I would initiate a debate every time we had even the most minor disagreement (like, whether we should go to McDonald's or Wendy's). And with my sound arguments, clear logic, expert testimony, and sharp-tongued rebuttals, I would win! Every time! Hooray for me! But my wife was becoming increasingly unimpressed with my argumentative genius, and things were going downhill fast.

Then, one of my mentors recommended a book to me. One of the first self-help books I ever read - *How to Win Friends and Influence People* by Dale Carnegie.

"How to Win Friends?" I asked. "I don't need to read this. I have plenty of friends."

"Trust me, Jeff," he replied, "You need to read it."

I did, and I was mortified when I got to Part Three, Chapter 1 – "You Can't Win an Argument." I learned a perspective I had never even considered - *when two people argue, **nobody wins**.*

Let's say, for example, that you and I argued about something you have strong feelings about – abortion, gun control, climate change, whatever. If I was on the opposite side of those issues from you, what are the odds of me changing your mind? Zero, right? What do you think the odds are of you changing my mind? Zero.

What if I bring up arguments you have no rebuttal for or evidence you've never heard before? Are you going to say, "Ok, I guess I've been wrong this whole time"? Nope. You'll go home and research, read articles, watch videos, and find experts who agree. You'll dig in *even deeper into your existing beliefs*.

And you'll probably like and respect me a little less.

Or a lot less.

You don't "win" arguments; you only damage relationships.

So, I try my best not to argue with people. I know what I believe, and I'm happy to share it with interested people, but I won't debate you, in person, on social media, or anywhere else. Occasionally someone tries to pick an argument with me because they like the thrill of intellectual sparring, and I tell them I'd rather not debate with them. "Because you know you're wrong?" they invariably say. "No," I reply, "Because I value our friendship more than I value being right."

Change Your Reactions. One of the keys to communicating more effectively with difficult people is to take responsibility for your role in these dysfunctional relationships. Like my dad used to say when I was fighting with one of my brothers, and we were both claiming the other started it, "It takes two to tango." (I had no idea what that meant when I was a kid).

In one of the best-named books I've read, *Since Strangling Isn't an Option...*, Sandra Crowe said, "Before you decide what you're going to do to fix things, you must really look inside and take responsibility for the situation, your role in it, and your reaction to it. The key to success with difficult people is in changing your response to them."

You gain power and control when you take full responsibility for your actions and reactions. I sometimes ask my audiences, "Raise your hand if someone did something to make you angry in the last six months." Everyone always raises their hand. "Someone *made* you angry?" I challenge. "They *MADE* you? Who are these people that you've put in charge of your emotions? And why would you do that? I bet you don't even *like* those people!"

Here's the truth – *no one* has the power to *MAKE* you angry. What happened is that someone did something you didn't like, and you chose anger as your response. You *chose*. Now, maybe you've been choosing anger as your go-to response every time something didn't go your way, every day for years, and now it's a habit – and habits are hard to break – but it's still a choice. When you accept that, you've set yourself free.

One area I used to struggle with was dealing with *critical people*. I have a sanguine personality type, which means I'm outgoing and the life of the party, but it also means I tend to be overly sensitive to criticism. For decades, whenever someone would criticize me, I would overreact and attack them verbally, criticizing them right back. I hurt many feelings, damaged many relationships, and always felt horrible after those conversations. I was embarrassed about what they said about me and what I said about them. It was a double whammy to my ego.

One day, I picked up and read a short, simple book called *The How to Easily Handle Difficult People Handbook* by Murray Oxman. And I mean short. The book is 16 pages. I think I found it on a spinning rack in an airport gift shop. In that book, I found some advice that changed my life. He recommended that the next time someone criticizes you, to agree with them. I thought this was bizarre advice, but I decided to try it.

The next time a critic came after me, I said, "That's an interesting point. It gives me something to think about. Thank you."

Disarmed, he said, "Oh. Ok. Good."

I've used that line **hundreds of times**. I let people get off their chest whatever bothers them, and then I live my life however I choose. It's a beautiful thing!

By the way, if you hate this book and write me a critical email – here's a preview of how I will respond: "That's an interesting point. That gives me something to think about. Thank you." I just saved you some time!

Something I've learned along the way is that when people spend their time and energy attacking and criticizing others – it says way more about them than it does about the person they are attacking. If you have kids on social media, you may want to teach them that.

So, by understanding what difficult people are, why they behave the way they do, and learning some strategies to communicate with them more effectively, I hope you feel better prepared to deal with the people in your life who cause you stress.

Hopefully, the time you spend around difficult people is limited and sporadic. The next topic we'll explore is how to better communicate *with the people you spend the most time with*.

CHAPTER 28

COMMUNICATING IN YOUR RELATIONSHIPS

Good communication is part of every relationship. All relationships have ups and downs and bumps in the road, but learning how to communicate more effectively will put you in a position to handle conflict better when it arises and have healthier friendships and partnerships.

I cherish and take pride in some profoundly gratifying, solid lifelong relationships. For example, my wife Kathy and I just celebrated our 32nd wedding anniversary. Our marriage is by no means perfect, but we've been loving and supporting each other and making it work for more than a billion seconds!

I've also had relationships that fell apart. I've had friends and family members whom I've distanced myself from because they frequently lied, acted too selfishly and erratically, or were dangerous to be around.

But many friendships I've lost over my lifetime were my fault. I said or did something that diminished trust, made a joke that I thought was funny but was deeply hurtful to someone else, took someone for granted, or got so focused on my own life that good friends just faded away. I regret it, and I've learned some lessons from it.

Relationships are important. Belgian psychotherapist and relationship expert Esther Perel says, "The quality of our relationships determines the quality of our lives."

So, in this chapter, let's dig into some ideas about improving how you communicate with the people you care about.

INVEST IN PRESENCE

There is power in just "being there" for someone. I have friends who I know would be there for me if I needed them or were in trouble, and I think the more of those you have, the better you sleep at night. And there are many people I'd be there for, too, if they needed me. The same is true for your spouse. Being there, often and open, to provide what that person needs is crucial.

We live in a time when it's never been easier to fill every moment of your day with activities, work, hobbies, interests, and entertainment. It's easy to let your loved ones get squeezed out. Do you go to work, give your best, and then come home with only your "leftover" energy? Giving your spouse the doggy-bag level leftover energy and attention chips away at intimacy and connection. Be present for the people who mean the most to you.

LEARN TO LISTEN

There is a lot about listening in this book, which may surprise you from a book entitled "Say It." But listening is one of the most crucial elements of effective communication. As I covered in Chapter 21, when you listen to people, you discover what is important to them. And when you listen to someone, it ***does*** "say" something – that you respect and value them.

Just like there are different speaking strategies based on the setting and audience, there are different listening strategies, too. The two main ones are *listening to respond* and *listening to understand*.

Listening to Respond. This type of listening is used in problem-solving. Depending on your profession, you may be called upon to resolve a situation, fix a problem, or develop a plan to move forward in a new direction. When listening to respond, someone looks to you for advice, guidance, or leadership. You're gathering facts and developing a strategy, but the purpose of the conversation is focused on taking action. This listening comes naturally to many entrepreneurs, managers, parents, husbands, and coaches. It's the listening I am personally most comfortable with. In my mind, I have a solution to every problem! I'm a superhero who can come to the rescue and fix any situation!

However, there are other kinds of listening, and using *listening to respond* in many situations worsens things.

Listening to Understand. The goal of listening to understand is not to solve a problem but to show empathy. This type of listening isn't focused on strategies and solutions but on the individual you are speaking with. You're listening to help that person feel better about themselves, their situation, and their peace of mind.

To effectively listen to understand, you must be willing and able to put yourself in the other person's shoes. You listen entirely, without interrupting, and read between the lines for what isn't being said. It doesn't mean you agree with everything the person says, but it shows that you care. People often just want to be heard and know their feelings aren't crazy. You must resist the urge to say, "Here's what you should do . . ." because this type of listening isn't about you and your solutions; it's about the other person and their needs. Few things can draw people closer together and enhance feelings of love and respect more than when someone effectively listens to understand.

Listening to understand may seem less heroic because comic books are not full of stories about great listeners. Still, it can increase your chances of developing happy, healthy relationships.

How do you know which type of listening to use? The best way is to ask the person you're talking to! A powerful question is, "Would you like me to help you brainstorm solutions to your problem, or do you just need someone to listen?" In my marriage, it's about 80% "I just need someone to listen."

SPEAK THE RIGHT LANGUAGE

One of the books that changed my life came out in 1992, just in time, one year after my wife and I got married. It's called *The Five Love Languages* by Gary Chapman. The idea is that people feel love in different ways, and if you understand what makes others feel loved, you can more effectively communicate love in a way that speaks to their hearts. I recommend you read the book, especially if you are in, or plan to be in, a romantic relationship, but here is a quick overview of the Five Love Languages:

Words of Affirmation. These people feel loved when they get compliments, positive reinforcement, encouragement, and praise.

Quality Time. These people feel loved when they get undivided attention, and they want their loved ones to put down their cell phones and actively listen.

Physical Touch. Someone with this as their primary love language feels most loved through physical affection like hugs, holding hands, or a back rub after a long day.

Acts of Service. These people feel most loved when someone does something to help or serve them, and they notice whenever someone does something to make life easier for them.

Gifts. The person who responds to this Love Language interprets gift-giving as a sign of love and affection. They value the present and the time that went into getting it.

After my wife and I read and discussed this book, we realized that *my* primary love languages were *Words of Affirmation* and *Physical Touch*. I feel loved when she tells me how awesome I am and hugs me.

Her primary love languages were *Acts of Service* and *Quality Time*. It was as if we were literally speaking different languages, like German and Chinese; neither knew what the other was "saying," nor were we getting what we needed. I was trying to make her feel loved by telling her I loved her and giving her big hugs, which she could take or leave.

She was trying to make me feel loved by doing acts of service like taking out the trash or taking my suits to the dry cleaner, which I barely noticed or appreciated because that's not my love language! We both had great intentions but didn't understand each other's needs well enough to communicate effectively.

Interestingly, we'd both buy gifts for each other, thinking we should, but neither of us responds to the love language of **Gifts**. When either of us would buy the other a gift, the recipient would think, "How much did that cost?" and then return it to the store.

One night, after we read that book, Kathy was very tired after work and said, "I am so behind on laundry, but I'm exhausted and just don't have the energy. I'm going to bed." I thought, Ah-ha! An opportunity to show her how much I love her in a way that speaks to her heart. Acts of Service to the rescue! I stayed up all night, did five loads of laundry, something I had never done before, and carefully folded each item of clothing and stacked it all neatly on the couch in our little apartment. When Kathy woke up and saw that, she started to cry. "I can't believe you did that for me!" she said. Remarkable, I thought, because it had never occurred to me to look at laundry as something she *was doing for me* because we are wired differently.

So, I challenge you to learn about your needs and those of the others you care about. I've found this helpful in the workplace and business teams, too. Some people need more praise and gratitude, while others would feel loved and appreciated if you gave them a $5 gift card for ice cream. If you do that to manipulate people, you're a terrible person. But if you do it to show people they are valued and make them feel special – that's leadership.

BE SMART ABOUT THE WORDS YOU USE

One of the things you learn fast when you start a relationship is what words and phrases don't go over well. Everyone is different, but I recommend avoiding using words like "always" and "never" – "You always do that," or "You never help with . . ." It probably isn't true, and over-generalizing damages relationships.

When things get tense, never say, "Calm down." Ever. That's certain to backfire. Never in the history of calming down has telling someone to calm down made them calm down.

Be careful with sarcasm and poking fun at them, even if you're "just kidding." Even if the person laughs, deep down, you've sparked some doubt, anxiety, fear, or other emotion.

I love Stephen Covey's concept of an **emotional bank account**. The idea is that you start with a zero balance with every new relationship you have. You make deposits into that account or withdrawals with each interaction. When you encourage, praise, are grateful, apologize, keep your promises, or show integrity, you are making deposits into that relationship. You are making withdrawals when you criticize, lie, betray, are sarcastic, fail to follow through, or lose your temper. When there are more deposits than withdrawals, you have a healthy account balance with that person. When the withdrawals exceed the deposits, that account will be overdrawn, and that relationship will eventually be closed.

TELL PEOPLE HOW YOU FEEL ABOUT THEM

One of the best ways to grow an emotional bank account is to tell the people you care about how you feel about them. Often. You may not have grown up in a family that expressed love frequently, but that's not an excuse. Do it. I tell my wife and kids that I love them *all the time*, and tell my friends and business partners, too.

I had a close friend for 18 years named Tim. He was one of my college students who asked me to help him start his own business. I did, and over time we became close friends. Like many great relationships, it was rooted in the fact that we were working together to make a difference in other people's lives. We had very different personalities and had to work to figure out how to communicate effectively, strengthening our relationship over time. He often told me he looked at me as a brother. I have lots of brothers, but there is always room for more! One terrible day, I got the call that Tim had suddenly and unexpectedly died at 36. It was one of the hardest things I've ever gone through. But I was so glad that the last time we spoke, Tim and I told each other how much we appreciated each other, and I told him I loved him. It gives me so much peace knowing that it didn't go unsaid. Tell the people you love that you love them. It will improve relationships, and you never know when it will be too late.

TEAR DOWN THAT WALL

In relationships, you must be watchful so that walls don't build up between you and others. When you don't have meaningful communication with someone for a while, I've noticed that a metaphorical wall starts to appear between you and them. You begin to wonder if they care about you. You start questioning their motives. You make assumptions about what they think or feel. You hear something they said to another person and wonder if they were talking about you. The wall grows taller and thicker, and the relationship starts to die.

This happened to me with one of my best friends. We've been close friends for decades, and he's done a lot for me. But as close as we are, a wall snuck in between us. And it started with a small withdrawal from our shared emotional bank account.

Probably ten years ago, someone told me they had heard him talking about me behind my back. That's it. Little thing, right? But it surprised me. It bothered me. It made me question whether we were friends or just acquaintances. It made me question if I could trust him. I started judging him a little: He's not so great. Who does he think he is? I've done a lot for him, too, you know! I started distancing myself; I didn't call or text for a while and declined invitations to get together. And my anger, bitterness, and resentment grew. I was holding a grudge, and it was getting heavy.

He could tell something was wrong, so he invited me to lunch. I had some choices: 1) Blow it off and decline the invite, 2) Go to lunch and pretend everything is fine, or 3) Confront him about what I heard he said and see what he says.

I decided on option 3. Even though the funds in our emotional bank account were declining, there was still a healthy balance from decades of goodwill. So, I told him what I had heard he had said and what I thought about it.

Now *he* had a choice on how to handle it: 1) Deny it, 2) Admit it, but play it off as no big deal, 3) Admit it and apologize. I didn't know what he would do, and I was ready to walk away from the friendship based on his response.

He chose option 3. He admitted what he had said and apologized profusely. He gave a genuine apology, by the way. Not the "Apology-Lite" that I hear a lot. Here's Apology-Lite: "I'm sorry that you're upset." That is *not* a genuine apology! A real apology is "I was wrong. I'm sorry. Please forgive me. I won't do it again."

He apologized, and we got our friendship back on track. I didn't automatically trust him again immediately, though. Trust is tricky – it takes a long time to earn and can be lost instantly. But trust *can be* re-earned. And he has. We are back to being close friends; everything is A-Okay, and our friendship is stronger now that it has been accidentally damaged and purposely repaired. So, when you feel those walls creeping up, if you value the relationship, tear them down!

This gives you some good things to consider as you learn to communicate better in your relationships. You may want to return to this chapter often and inventory your relationships.

The next chapter will focus on what can be one of the most challenging and rewarding types of relationships you could have – *as parents*.

CHAPTER 29

COMMUNICATING AS PARENTS

Of all the different types of conversations you'll have in your life, it's hard to think of many that will be more important or have longer-lasting effects than the ones you will have if you have kids. Of all the unique and interesting roles I have played in my life, there is none that I have enjoyed more or am more proud of than my role of Dad. Being a parent is equal parts challenging, rewarding, terrifying, and thrilling. I hope being a professional communicator has made me a better parent, and I *know* being a parent has made me a better communicator.

We have three adult offspring. They are 24, 21, and 18 at the time of this writing. The last quarter-century has been the greatest of my life, filled with amazing adventures and profound lessons. In this chapter, I will share what I've learned about communicating with kids as you shepherd them safely into adulthood. We aren't perfect parents, but we have learned some things!

TALK WITH THEM EVERY DAY

I didn't say talk **to** them but **with** them. There's a lot of "talking to" that happens every day – "Please clean your room," "Did you do your homework?" "Time for bed!" That will happen a lot. But what will make a massive difference as they grow up are the *real conversations*. We always wanted our kids to feel comfortable coming to us with their questions, fears, doubts, and insecurities when they were teenagers, so we prioritized having conversations with them from the time they could talk.

If you make daily communication a habit for you and your kids, they are more likely to talk to you when a crisis hits or they have an embarrassing experience. As I covered in the last chapter, frequent communication keeps the walls from going up. We'd talk, not just about what was going on in their lives, but *how they felt about it*. That's where connection happens, and that's where you build trust.

I learned a powerful lesson about being present when my daughter Natalie was three. I was spending some "quality family time" sitting on the couch, answering emails on my laptop. "Quality family time" is in quotations because it's a dubious claim, as I was 100% focused on what I was doing on my laptop. I just happened to be in the room with some of my kids. Little three-year-old Natalie came up to me and said, "Hey, Daddy, listen to me."

"What is it, honey? I'm listening," I replied, still totally focused on the computer screen and typing away.

She climbed onto the couch, stepped over my lap, and sat on the laptop keyboard. She took my face in both hands and turned my face directly toward hers.

186

"No, Daddy," she said, "Listen with your *eyes*."

I learned more about communication at that moment *from a toddler* than I did from a master's degree in Communication. That's when I realized that if you're not looking at someone, you're not listening. And you're not being present, even in the same room.

SET STANDARDS, NOT RULES

One of the most essential parenting lessons I learned surprisingly came from a college basketball coach. I've always been a fan of legendary basketball coach Mike Krzyzewski from Duke University. Eleven years ago, I was invited to a charity fundraiser at Duke, where the attendees got to sit in on a closed-door private practice, have dinner with Coach K, listen to him teach and share with the group, and ask questions. It was a fantastic day. I learned more about teamwork, leadership, excellence, mentoring, and winning in one day with a great coach than in five years of college and two degrees! (If you want to see a video about that day, including clips I filmed of Coach K speaking, head over to my YouTube channel "An Epic Life.")

My biggest takeaway was his explaining how there were no rules in his program, no rules but *high standards*. I honestly didn't know the difference, but he explained. Nobody likes rules. The people being "ruled" don't like it, don't believe in the rules, and understandably resist. A leader who spends all their time enforcing rules isn't a leader at all. *Standards*, however, are something everyone can get behind. Standards are things to which *we all hold each other accountable*. Rules make people feel limited and controlled, but high standards inspire people to do better and be better. It's a profound concept.

After I learned that from Coach K, my wife and I started talking less about rules and punishments with our kids and more about our family standards. Things like: We encourage each other, we forgive each other, we treat everyone with kindness, we stand up for people who can't stand up for themselves, and we are always honest with each other. Our kids never got into much trouble, and I credit Coach K and his wisdom for a lot of that.

ENCOURAGE YOUR KIDS TO FAIL

I often do training on the power of failure. People have an enormous misconception thinking that failure is the opposite of success. That hasn't been my experience at all! Everything I do well today, I used to do poorly. But with practice and coaching, I got better and eventually succeeded. Failure isn't the *opposite* of success; it's the *precursor* to success. Always. You *must* fail before you succeed.

The problem with believing failure is the opposite of success is that people who believe that will avoid failure at all costs. And people who are afraid to fail *never even try*.

Henry Ford said, "Failure is the opportunity to begin again more intelligently." According to Winston Churchill, "Success consists of going from failure to failure without loss of enthusiasm." Failing is one of the most instructive, essential things you could do. It's wise to encourage your kids to *try, fail, think, adjust, and try again*. If they don't, how will they ever grow into strong adults?

One of the best examples of the power of failure I've seen was from my daughter Amanda. When she was seven years old, she started taking karate classes at our local YMCA. She enjoyed it, and I liked that she was developing things like speed, power, coordination, balance, and coachability – which could benefit her no matter what other sports she decided to play. But she stuck with it and decided that karate was her thing.

About two years in, as she steadily advanced up the belts on her way to Black Belt, she was invited to join a select competitive fighting team with her dojo. This meant not just taking classes and tests but *competing* against kids from other karate dojos. She went to a local tournament and got a gold medal! Yes! Then a regional tournament and a gold medal! State Championship and another gold medal! She was crushing it.

Her team then attended the USA National Karate Championships in Houston, Texas. Before the tournament, I asked her what her goal was. She said, "Dad, I want to win a ***gold medal*** at nationals. I want to be a ***National Champion***!" It sounded good to me!

When I tell this story to audiences, I ask them to guess what place she came in out of around 20 kids, who were all at her same age and belt level.

"1st place!" someone always shouts. Nope.

"2nd?" No.

She came in almost last place. She was crushed. I was devastated for her. I wanted that gold medal for her more than I've ever wanted anything for myself! I will never forget her telling me with tears in her eyes, "It's the first time I ever failed." Yep. It's rough. But it's part of the journey to being a champion.

So, she trained and worked hard for another year and returned to nationals the following year in Florida. I asked her what her goal was. "First place. Gold medal. National champion," she said. She competed in several events, and in one of them, she won a *bronze medal!*

I ask the audience when telling this story, "Bronze medal - Success or failure?" And they all yell out, "**Success!**"

"You people aren't very good with numbers, are you?" I reply. "Her *goal* was *first place*, and she got *third place*. She failed. She improved, but she failed. She failed to hit her goal."

Boy, do I get dirty looks from people in the audience when I say that. Someone, usually a mom or grandma, angrily shouts, "Don't you dare call that girl a failure!"

"Whoa!" I say, "I never said she **WAS** a failure. I said she *failed*. Failure is an event, not a person."

Let me repeat that. *Failure is an event; it's not a person.* A person *can't be* a failure. You can't *be a failure* any more than you could be Christmas Eve or the Super Bowl. Those are *events*.

She failed. If you think that's a terrible thing to say, you don't understand what failure is and isn't.

It was a failure. An amazing failure! A beautiful failure! An instructive failure.

By the way, do you think I was any prouder of her because she won a medal than I was the year before? Of course not. I was proud every time she stepped out on that mat to compete, risking getting punched in the face and getting judged for it. It's a courageous thing to do!

Her goal was to win gold the following year, but she won a **bronze and a silver medal**. Another awesome failure!

In the fourth year, she won **gold** in two events! **Success**! She hit her goal! National Champion!

The fifth year she repeated as National Champion with another gold medal. Her dreams had come true. But they wouldn't have without the failures, **which are always part of the process**. Today Amanda is a strong, confident woman. She's a licensed Interpreter for the Deaf, and interestingly, those precise, fluid hand movements she learned in those karate katas help her do what she does with excellence!

She failed her way to success, just like every person who has ever succeeded in anything. How you communicate about failure in your home will significantly impact your kids' future chances of reaching their goals and dreams.

CATCH 'EM DOING THINGS RIGHT

One of the lessons I've learned about **driving change** in human behavior is that you get better results when you praise someone for doing something right than correcting them for doing things wrong. Part of wise communication in parenting is praising, encouraging, and complimenting when they do something well. If your kid does something the wrong way 9 out of 10 times, be patient, and pour on the recognition and edification the one time they do it the way you want. See if they don't start doing better than 9 out of 10.

PUT YOUR KIDS IN A POSITION TO BE PROUD OF THEMSELVES

Every human being loves to stay in their comfort zone. It's comfortable in there! As a parent, you must work a difficult balance: You want to protect your children physically and emotionally, but you also know that growth takes place outside that comfort zone. You must encourage your kids to leave their comfort zone without pushing them out. They have to do it themselves.

Our son Logan is an extraordinary dude. When he was around seven, he took an interest in roller coasters that became an obsession. He'd spend hours watching YouTube videos and memorizing the stats – what year each coaster opened, the manufacturer, the height, maximum speed, etc. But he was afraid to ride.

We'd bring him to our local amusement park, Kings Island, for a whole summer to watch the roller coasters. I encouraged him to ride, talking about the safety features and trying to get him to see how proud he would be if he rode some coasters. Firm no.

One June day the following summer, when he was eight, he said, "Dad, I'm ready to be brave." We went over to Kings Island, and he conquered his fears and rode the kiddie coaster Snoopy's Flying Ace Ariel Chase! The first thing he said when he got off was, "**I'm so proud of myself!**" I was proud of him, but there is something so empowering when someone faces and overcomes their fears and is proud of *themselves*.

Logan rode every ride in the park that summer, including some 200-foot-tall coasters. The following year, he started traveling with me when I spoke at events around the country, and we would go to amusement parks and ride coasters together. He started his own YouTube channel to share his passion called ***Koaster Kids***, and I supported and helped him by filming and editing his videos.

Long story short, the channel blew up, and Logan made friends and connected with fans worldwide. The channel reached over 30,000 subscribers, and Logan has now ridden over 550 roller coasters in 8 countries. He has helped hundreds of other kids overcome their fears of heights and coasters. This adventure has helped him develop exceptional communication and social skills, learn to work with the media, run a small business, and handle online haters and critics. He now works at Kings Island in the Rides Department, running the same roller coasters that he used to be afraid of and training new hires, and he's well on his way to a career in the amusement industry. Today, he's a confident man, a great teammate, a loyal friend to people, and a good person. I'm so proud of him and glad we encouraged him, gently and constantly, to face those fears and earn his own respect!

BE HONEST

Surprisingly, this one is controversial when I talk about it at conferences. I recommend that when communicating with your kids, ***you should be honest***.

Even when it's hard.

Especially when it's hard.

I don't think you have any credibility when you ask your kids to be honest if you're not honest too. Punishing them for lying when you lie to your kids is about as hypocritical as it gets.

Here's an example that's certain to step on some toes: This is why we never lied to our kids about Santa Claus, the Easter Bunny, or the Tooth Fairy. It didn't seem right for me to string them along for years, asking them to put faith in these beings they couldn't see and then yank the rug out from under them. So, we didn't do the lying part. We told our kids that those were *characters* like Sponge Bob or Spiderman. They add some fun to the holidays, but they are fictional.

The part of the Santa scam that always bothered me the most was the manipulative "naughty or nice" part. If you're good, Santa will bring you presents; if you're bad, he'll bring you a lump of coal. That's pretty twisted.

We told our kids that their gifts came from their parents, not a creepy North Pole based behavior-tracking spy program, and they were an expression of *our unconditional love*, not a reward for being nice. Incidentally, this better aligned with my spiritual belief that MY heavenly Father shows me unconditional love, even when I've been naughty. I don't think those holidays were any less magical and fun for our kids than for the kids who were duped into believing those characters were real.

You wouldn't believe the number of people who have attacked me for not playing along with the mythical character scam. It fascinates me because it is such shaky moral ground to be upset at someone for being honest with their kids. You do what you want. I'm just giving you something to think about.

TEACH YOUR KIDS TO TELL STORIES

Some dads teach their kids how to fish, rebuild a carburetor, or pitch a tent, but I don't know how to do any of those things. I taught my kids the valuable skill of *storytelling*.

When my daughter Natalie was four and five, we would snuggle at bedtime and play the Story Game. I would name three unrelated things, and then she would have to make up a story. I'd say, "Ok, a trombone, a monkey, and a calendar." She would say (and you should read this in your head in the voice of a cute little girl), "Once upon a time, there was a monkey named Edgar who found a calendar, and he was very sad. He saw in the calendar that there was going to be a concert, but he didn't have any instruments to play . . ." She would create and tell the most elaborate, detailed stories, filled with compelling characters pursuing meaningful goals, overcoming hardship and conflict, and the story would always end, ". . . and they lived happily ever after!"

Fast-forward, Natalie is still an extraordinary speaker. She crushed her high school speech class and is now in college, studying to be a high school teacher. She lights up the room when she speaks to an audience and radiates passion and enthusiasm. She's also highly emotionally intelligent, adroitly navigating relationships and helping others. I'm super proud of her, and I love thinking back to the Story Game when she was just a wee lass!

I don't think many parents have storytelling on the list of skills they want to teach their kids, but I know what a crucial skill it is. Potentially more valuable than anything they're going to learn in school.

I could tell you a thousand other stories about what I've learned raising these great kids, but I won't. Hopefully, these recommendations get your wheels turning about ways to communicate more effectively with your kids.

Well, there is one chapter left, and it's about communicating with *a very important individual ...*

CHAPTER 30

COMMUNICATING TO YOURSELF

I can't end a book about communicating with power, effectiveness, and authenticity without addressing the person you talk to most often and with whom your words have the most influence and impact – **you**.

As I covered in Chapter 3, you are a spirit, have a soul (your mind, will, emotions), and live in a body. I'm convinced that your spirit connects with others, but your mind determines what you believe, do, and think about.

HOW YOUR MIND WORKS

Humans have a conscious and a subconscious mind. Your **conscious** mind is where you process information. It includes anything in your current awareness. It's thoughts, feelings, sensations, fantasies, perceptions, and memories. It's where you observe, worry, contemplate, obsess, and think about what you want for dinner. Your conscious mind gets tired throughout the day and sleeps when your body does.

You also have a **subconscious** mind which is the non-analytical, always-on part of your mind that acts as storage. Your entire life, it's been collecting and storing feelings, thoughts, fears, and beliefs that come from your conscious mind. Over time, your subconscious mind manifests what you feed it, converting ideas into firmly held convictions, driving your habits, actions, and reactions.

It's vital that you understand that your subconscious mind **believes everything**, and it has no way of distinguishing between what is good and evil or what is true or untrue. **It's like soil.** When a seed is planted, soil anchors the plant's roots and provides moisture and nutrients. Soil cannot differentiate corn or blueberry seeds from thistle or poison ivy seeds. It provides all of them a place to grow and thrive.

THE PROBLEM

Unfortunately, many thoughts and ideas planted in the fertile soil of your subconscious mind over your lifetime are more like ragweed and kudzu than they are orchids and daffodils. Many ideas about the world and yourself that your subconscious mind believes and uses to drive your behavior aren't healthy or valuable, and many aren't even true.

Some wrong ideas are **things other people told you or taught you**; you are "less than," worthless, dumb, ugly, or not good enough. That getting what you want out of life is impossible, or selfish, or materialistic. That happiness and success are for other people, not you. Author and speaker Jen Sincero says: "Most people are living in an illusion based on someone else's beliefs."

But *what you have told yourself* is even more damaging than what others have told you or said about you. Psychologist Gloria Waite said, "Your subconscious mind saves it all. All the things you tell yourself (and have told yourself in the past) are stored in your subconscious mind, and it accepts them as real, as the truth. And even more importantly, it takes on your interpretation of the facts, which may not be totally objective!"

Throughout your life, you've told yourself negative, horrible things:

"Bad things always happen to me."
"I'll never find someone who loves me for who I am."
"The world would be better off without me."
"My life is a dumpster fire."
"I can't do anything right."
"Good things never last."
"I hate my body."
"Everything I touch turns into trash."
"I'm just a hot mess."
"I hate my life."
"This just isn't my day."
"I always freeze up in front of a crowd."
"No one cares what I think."
"This business just won't work for me."

Those thoughts have seeped into your subconscious mind and taken root. They've poisoned your future and sabotaged your chances of happiness, success, and fulfillment.

In his book *The Power of Your Subconscious Mind*, Joseph Murphy said, "All that we achieve as well as all that we fail to achieve is the direct result of our own thoughts. Our weaknesses and strengths, purity and impurity, are ours alone. They can only be altered by us; never by another. All our happiness and suffering are evolved from within. As we think, so we are; as we continue to think, so we remain."

So, what do you do?

UNLEARN

The first step is to start working to identify the lies and misconceptions you have accepted your whole life. How do you do that? I found that being wiser about my association helped. When I started hanging around positive, successful, happy people with passion and purpose driving them, I quickly noticed they talked about different things than I did. They were **positive** - not "happy all the time" - they were *positive* they would win, *positive* nothing could stop them. They talked more about the future than the past. They didn't rip each other all the time; they uplifted others and celebrated other people's successes instead of being petty and jealous.

It was different than what I was used to. I started contrasting what they believed about themselves and the world to what I felt about myself and the world and began identifying flaws in my thought process and the negative roots of my way of thinking. It was like having corrupted files removed from a computer.

I could give you hundreds of examples, but here's a big one: I struggled with networking and talking to strangers when starting my own business. I knew I didn't have enough contacts to build a successful company and would have to get aggressive about networking with people I didn't know. But I was paralyzed by a fear of what they would think of me. I didn't want to look stupid, too pushy, or weird. I'd lay in bed at night thinking about what a loser I was.

Then one day, it dawned on me what negative seed had been planted in my subconscious mind that had grown into a monster. It was something I had heard over and over when I was little that had seeped into my operating system and corrupted all the files:

Don't talk to strangers.

When I was growing up, I was repeatedly told by people in authority, "Don't talk to strangers." So, my subconscious mind treated talking to strangers with the same danger and fear as "Don't play in traffic" and "Don't drink and drive." The mere thought of talking one-on-one to a stranger triggered a fearful fight or flight response. The weird thing is that I had no problem talking to large audiences full of strangers. Thank God my teachers never taught me, "Don't talk to audiences!"

Once I realized what was happening in my head, I started working to unlearn what I had learned as a kid. I thought about the truth related to this topic:

✦ You can't be successful in any career without talking to strangers.

✦ Talking to strangers isn't dangerous. They're not going to hit me.

✦ Everyone I know now was a stranger once.

✦ Who cares what a stranger thinks of me?

The more I thought about it, the sillier the whole idea was. I resolved to talk to more strangers, become skillful at talking to strangers, and change some strangers' lives *because* I spoke to them! And you can be sure; I *never* told my kids not to talk to strangers. I taught them: Don't get in a car with a stranger and don't take anything a stranger offers you, but you should be nice and kind to everyone you meet, especially strangers!

I've worked hard to unlearn many self-limiting thought processes holding me back, and I'm still working on it. You will need to as well. This is not a new idea I made up, by the way. Two thousand four hundred years ago, Greek philosopher Antisthenes, a student of Socrates, wrote, "The most useful piece of learning for the uses of life is to unlearn what is untrue."

More recently, 1970's "futurist" Alvin Toffler, author of influential books like *Future Shock* and *The Third Wave*, wrote, "The illiterate of the future will not be those who cannot read or write, but those who cannot learn, unlearn, and relearn."

UTILIZE POSITIVE SELF-TALK

Thinking about these things and making new decisions can be helpful, but I've learned that the real power is in *your words*. You don't defeat thoughts with thoughts – you defeat thoughts with words. Saying things to yourself to change your subconscious mind is called self-talk.

In his book, *What To Say When You Talk to Yourself*, Dr. Shad Helmstetter said, "Self-talk is a way to override our past negative programming by erasing or replacing it with conscious, positive new directions. Self-talk is a practical way to live our lives by active intent rather than by passive acceptance."

Some people think it sounds hokey or mystical when you start talking about the power of words to create your reality and shape your future, but I think it's 100% true. Words are a powerful creative force, and every great idea and invention started as just words. Your words about yourself and your life will either trap you or set you free.

There is an excellent metaphor in the Bible, in the book of James, about your words being like the tiny rudder that steers an enormous ship. Interestingly, ships have gotten much larger since James' day, but the rudder is still relatively small, making all the difference in *setting direction*.

It's helpful to think happy thoughts, but nothing matches the productive power of speaking positive words of confidence, belief, and faith out loud. Many studies have shown that talking to yourself out loud increases focus, moves you toward your goals, and combats self-criticism.

This chapter is called "Communicating *To* Yourself" instead of "Communicating *With* Yourself" because you need to tell your subconscious mind what's what. That subconscious mind of yours needs a good talking to!

I frequently write down and then speak out loud statements about myself and my life that align with whom I want to be and where I want to go. Sometimes I remind my subconscious mind about things I know to be true. Sometimes I'm programming my mind to believe in things that haven't happened yet, calling into being things that don't yet exist.

By way of example, here are some of the positive self-talk statements I have used to start creating the life I want and to become the person I want to be. Don't copy these – come up with your own – but catch the idea. I speak in the present tense as if I already am everything I want to be and already have the things I want:

✦ There is nothing I can't accomplish if I focus and work smart.

✦ My company is growing every single month.

✦ I'm a credible, reliable example for the people I mentor.

✦ Sharp, teachable individuals and couples join my business team every day.

✦ Every day I look for ways to make Kathy's life better.

✦ I put other people's needs ahead of my own.

✦ People who hear me speak make breakthroughs in their lives.

✦ I add value to the lives of everyone I meet.

✦ My book makes a positive difference in the lives of readers.

✦ The future is brighter than the past.

✦ I consistently show unconditional love to my kids.

✦ I am developing leaders who can change their own worlds.

✦ I choose humility over pride and faith over fear.

✦ I live every day with passion and purpose.

✦ I am so thankful.

✦ I can do all things through Christ, who gives me strength.

I could share a hundred more, but you get the idea. I'm convinced that talking to myself this way has made a tremendous difference in my quality of life, peace of mind, the things I've accomplished, and my accomplishments yet to come!

Speak words of *life*, *hope*, *truth*, *and love*. Speak words that connect with what you want out of life. Align the words with your values, beliefs, dreams, and goals. Speak about who you really are, not the imposter you think you should portray.

If you haven't tried adding positive self-talk to your daily routine, I challenge you to try it. I double-dog-dare you. Now you have to do it.

I'll end this chapter with a great passage I read from author Omar Itani in his newsletter, *The Optimist*:

"You have the power to realize your self-worth and build up your confidence. You have the power to understand yourself better, to outline your goals, to conquer fear and become a more enthusiastic person on the path to achieving your dreams.

The key is to change the story you tell yourself.

Instead of regurgitating the same old narrative of believing you're not good enough to run your own business, you're too scared to travel alone, you'll only be happy once you're 20 pounds less, work on changing your inner monologue to: 'I can be successful in building my own business; I am brave to travel alone; I allow myself to live a happy life regardless of my circumstances.' Give yourself permission to be fearless, happy and prosperous. Give yourself permission to step into a mentally healthy and truly meaningful existence.

Unleash the power of your subconscious mind."

THE VERY END

So, there you have it! I packed in as much as possible into this book to help you learn to communicate with power, effectiveness, and authenticity. You've learned how to become a better public speaker, crush it when selling, and communicate in various crucial situations. I truly hope you found it practical, learned a lot, and your mind is spinning with new ideas, new strategies to implement, and new skills to work on.

I highly recommend creating *a personal action plan* based on what you learned from this book. What practical, daily activities will you add to your routine to ensure you develop the mindset and skill sets required to be a powerful communicator? If you have a mentor or business coach, share your action plan with them and ask them to hold you accountable. Make it a priority. If you don't take immediate action, the potential impact of the lessons in this book will fade away.

I'm sure you detected some common themes running through the sections and chapters of this book. I feel I should point out what I think the core theme of this book is:

If you want things to improve in your life, you need to take your eyes off yourself and focus on helping others.

It's the key to powerful public speaking, selling successfully, and communicating effectively with anyone. It's also the key to happiness. If you can learn to walk in love and selflessness, I'm confident you'll say it like it matters when it matters.

———————

Let me know if you are selecting a keynote speaker for a conference or have a business team you'd like me to speak for! I'd love to help you deliver impactful training for your attendees or team.

You can reach me at jeff@jeffjoiner.com
Check out my website at www.jeffjoiner.com
Find me on YouTube at "An Epic Life" www.youtube.com/anepiclife
Facebook – @JeffJoinerTraining
Instagram – @jeffreyjoiner
Twitter – @jeffjoiner

I'd love to hear from you if this book impacted you! Here's to your future of growing your influence as you communicate with power, effectiveness, and authenticity!

Milton Keynes UK
Ingram Content Group UK Ltd.
UKHW020645070923
428220UK00013B/493